AF722611

INFLATION AND UNEMPLOYMENT

INFLATION AND UNEMPLOYMENT

In the Modern Society

Thorkil Kristensen

PRAEGER

PRAEGER SPECIAL STUDIES • PRAEGER SCIENTIFIC

Library of Congress Cataloging in Publication Data

Kristensen, Thorkil, 1899
Inflation and unemployment.

Includes bibliographical references and index.
1. Economic policy. 2. Inflation (Finance)
3. Unemployment. 4. International economic relations. I. Title.
HD82.K76 338.9 80-22800
ISBN 0-03-057003-4

Published in 1981 by Praeger Publishers
CBS Educational and Professional Publishing
A Division of CBS, Inc.
521 Fifth Avenue, New York, New York 10017 U.S.A.

© 1981 by Praeger Publishers

All rights reserved

23456789 145 98765432

Printed in the United States of America

PREFACE

For the first time in history, an apparently persistent combination of inflation and unemployment has developed in modern Western societies. The oil price rises of the 1970s can explain only a minor part of the present difficulties that in fact began to appear long before the first of these price rises at the end of 1973.

There has been some inflation throughout the period since the end of World War II in 1945. It intensified in the middle of the 1960s, and during the last half of that decade it began to be combined with increasing rates of unemployment even though economic growth continued to be fairly rapid until the spring of 1973, when it stopped. At that time the international monetary system, based on fixed but adjustable exchange rates, also broke down as a consequence of disturbances that developed over a period of some years.

That all these changes could occur before the first oil price rise shows that there must be weaknesses in the ways in which the modern economic systems work. There is, therefore, a need to revise our thinking about these systems and in particular about the parts of economic theory that deal with inflation and unemployment. The present book is meant to be a contribution to this revision.

It so happens that the difficulties mentioned above developed during the period when the relations between the West and the other parts of the world were raising a number of new policy problems. Therefore, it has been necessary to look at the problems of the West in a global perspective. "The West" is to be understood here as the member countries of the Organization for Economic Cooperation and Development (OECD)—Western Europe, North America, Japan, Australia, and New Zealand. "The East" denotes the original members of COMECON, Eastern Europe and the USSR. By "the South" is meant the rest of the world. China is thus considered part of the South. Where the expression "the North" is used, it means the West and the East.

Chapter 1 describes how the present combination of inflation and unemployment has developed since the end of World War II. A comparison with the past is made in order to show in which ways the system works that are distinct from those in former times.

Chapter 2 deals with the complex system of organized markets, political activities, and other factors that characterizes modern societies. It is implied that this organization, more than anything else, explains why the economies behave in ways different from those of the past.

Chapter 3 deals with the inflation problem of today and its relations with the new ways the national economies function.

In a similar way Chapter 4 deals with the new tendency toward persistent unemployment. This problem is particularly complicated and also a politically difficult issue. Chapter 4 has a key position in the reasoning of the present book.

Chapter 5 deals with the relations among the various parts of the world, as they are related to the policy problems of the modern Western societies.

These policy problems are then dealt with more specifically in Chapter 6.

My thanks are due to Professors P. Norregaard Rasmussen and J. Tinbergen for valuable comments during the preparation of the study. Neither of them, however, is responsible for any of the views expressed in the book.

Thorkil Kristensen
Copenhagen
June 1980

CONTENTS

LIST OF TABLES

LIST OF FIGURES

INFLATION AND UNEMPLOYMENT

1 THE DEVELOPMENT OF INFLATION AND UNEMPLOYMENT

INFLATION

The unhappy combination of inflation and unemployment, which has characterized modern Western societies in recent years, is a new phenomenon. In former times prices went up and down during the business cycles. So did employment, but these were short-term fluctuations and there was neither persistent inflation nor persistent unemployment.

Inflation, sometimes even high rates of inflation, could occur during wars or revolutions, as can be seen from Figure 1.1, but when these disturbances were over, prices would fall to more or less the level before the conflict. It should be remembered that the figure describes wholesale prices, which usually show larger short-term fluctuations than consumer prices.

However, after World War I prices did not fall to the prewar level; the additional fall in prices during the Great Depression of the 1930s was short-lived; and after the inflation of World War II, prices did not fall at all. On the contrary, they continued to rise, especially in the countries that had taken part in the war, as can be seen from Table 1.1.

During the first postwar years, labor markets were tight in several countries. Many people had been killed or wounded, and reconstruction required much work. Also, there was a widespread tendency to pursue more expansionary economic policies than after World War I, in order to avoid unemployment. The influence of John Maynard Keynes, who had proposed such a policy, was beginning to be felt.[1] These policies were favorable to employment, but they also provoked rising wages and prices.

FIGURE 1.1: Wholesale Prices in the United States, 1770-1970

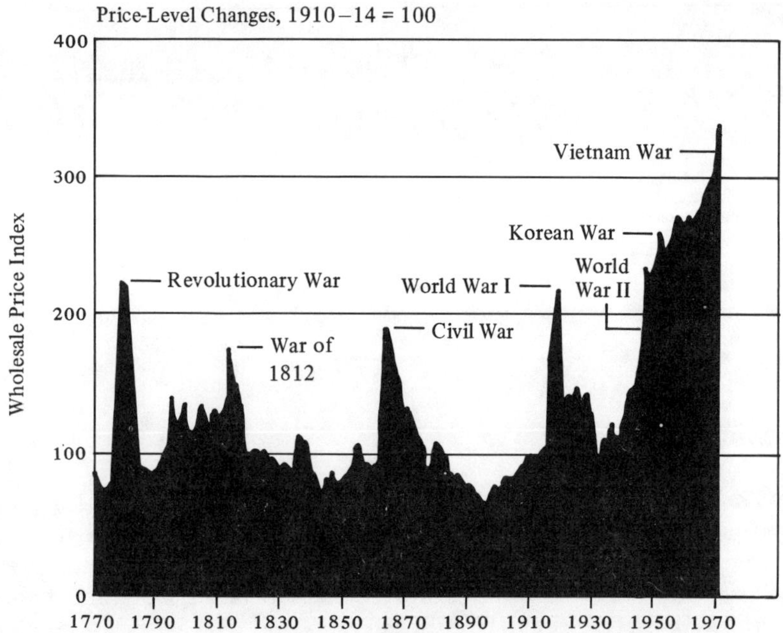

Source: Paul A. Samuelson, *Economics*, 9th ed. (New York: McGraw-Hill, 1973), p. 271. Used with the permission of McGraw-Hill Book Company.

Since 1950 the distinction between countries that had been at war and countries that had not has become less important. We can, therefore, look upon the West—what is now the OECD area—as a

TABLE 1.1: Consumer Price Indexes, 1945-50

	United Kingdom	*United States*	*West Germany*	*Sweden*	*Switzerland*
1945	—	75	75	93	93
1946	—	81	82	93	93
1947	94	93	87	96	97
1948	100	100	100	100	100
1949	103	99	107	102	99
1950	106	100	100	103	98

Source: *Statistical Yearbook of Denmark* (Copenhagen: The Statistical Department, 1955).

whole. The annual increase in consumer prices during the 1950s, according to the International Monetary Fund (IMF), was 3.0 percent from 1950 to 1955 and 2.5 percent from 1955 to 1960. The first part of the decade was, of course, marked by the Korean War.

After 1960 fairly expansionary policies were pursued in many countries. The rates of inflation therefore rose, especially after 1965. OECD statistics of consumer prices show the following annual increases:

Year(s)	*Percent*
1960-65	2.5
1965-68	3.4
1969-72	5.1
1973	8.0
1974	13.6
1975	11.4
1976-78	8.4
1979	9.9

The years 1973, 1974, and 1975 are shown separately because the first large oil price rise had some effect during the last months of 1973, whereas the full effect came in 1974. The price rises in 1974 and 1975 were partly due to the indirect consequences of this oil price rise, which reinforced the wage/price spiral that is characteristic of modern societies.

During 1976-78 oil prices were fairly stable, yet the rates of inflation were higher than before 1973. In 1979 oil prices were again raised substantially, and over the seven months June-December 1979, consumer prices rose at an annual rate of 11.9 percent.

It seems, then, that inflation has gradually become a persistent feature of modern economies. There has been some inflation during the entire postwar period and the annual rates of inflation have been increasing, at least since the last part of the 1960s.

The price rise experienced in the first part of this period could, to some extent, be said to be a result of the demand created by the financing of reconstruction and, more generally, a result of expansionary policies. The rates of inflation have, however, to an increasing extent continued to be high, even in years when the real price of oil has not increased and when economic growth has been slow.

This points to the conclusion that the economic systems are working in ways that differ from those of former times.

UNEMPLOYMENT

As already indicated, reconstruction after World War II and the policies pursued by many countries during the first part of the postwar period had a favorable effect on employment. Therefore, at least in many Western countries, the rates of unemployment were low during the first two decades after the war.

The West was even able to absorb an influx of labor from non-OECD countries, such as Mexico, North African countries, and Pakistan. This development, however, came to an end about the middle of the 1960s. Unemployment reached its lowest level in 1966, as can be seen from Figure 1.2.

Especially after 1969 unemployment increased, however, with the exception of the boom year 1972-73. At the same time, the rate of inflation also rose, as shown in the previous section, and the influx of foreign workers to the OECD area slowed down; in some cases it was even reversed.

When unemployment reached its low in 1966, it was just above 2 percent. For the period of rapid economic growth, 1960-73, the average rate of unemployment was 3.4 percent. Since then it has developed as shown below.[2]

Year(s)	*Percent*
1973-74	3.6
1974-75	5.3
1975-78	5.1
1980 (est.)	5.5

It seems that we have now entered a period of high rates of inflation combined with high rates of unemployment.

This is something new. During the first years after World War II, it was a widespread opinion, based partly on the reasoning of Keynes, that demand management through appropriate fiscal and monetary policies was the main instrument for ensuring a harmonious development. If the level of total demand was too low, there would be unemployment. If it was too high, there would be inflation. One therefore should steer a middle course.

But now we have inflation and unemployment at the same time. The main purpose of this study is to look into the questions of why that is so and what can be done about it. As an introduction it may be useful to compare the present period with the decades before World War I, when prices and employment fluctuated, but society was never locked in a situation similar to the apparently persistent combination of inflation and unemployment we have now.

FIGURE 1.2: Economic Growth and Unemployment in OECD Countries, 1960-78

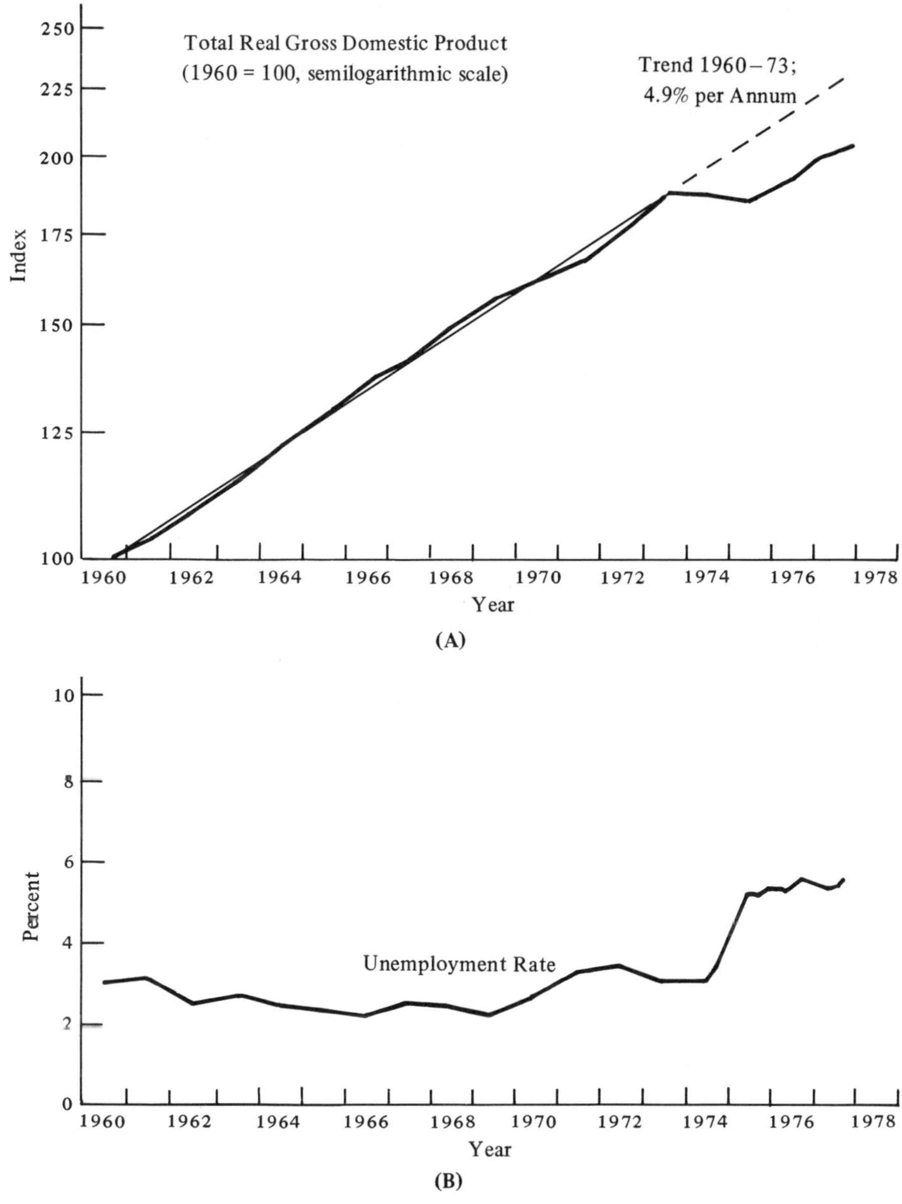

Source: Bank for International Settlements *Annual Report*, (Basel: Bank for International Settlements, 1978), p. 41.

COMPARISON WITH THE PAST

Why do modern economies of today function in ways that are different from those of former times? In order to answer that question, it is useful to look at the decades before World War I.* The more advanced Western societies were then increasingly becoming industrialized and the fluctuations called business cycles were becoming important. It is primarily investment that fluctuates during these cycles, and investment is to a large extent dominated by industry.

It is a characteristic feature of the business cycles of that period that prices, wages, and interest rates moved up and down, and so did employment, in a fairly regular way. Gustav Cassel has given a comprehensive description of the business cycles of the period from about 1870 to about 1910[3] Table 1.2 is a compilation of his small tables showing the years when prices, wages, rates of interest, and unemployment reached their highest and lowest points (max. and min.) during the various business cycles. The table is based on material covering the United Kingdom, which at that time was already a fairly advanced industrial country.

It will be seen that there was a remarkable degree of covariation. The prices of goods, labor, and capital reached their minimum and their maximum at more or less the same time. It is also evident that when the prices of these three factors went up, unemployment went down, and vice versa.

This is very important. It shows that strong forces of self-adjustment must have been at work. When the economy came close to an extreme situation—boom or depression—countervailing forces were already being provoked, so that a turning point was reached and both prices and employment began to move the other way. The system was not locked in a situation with a high rate of inflation or of unemployment, and certainly never with the two evils at the same time.

It is this capability of self-adjustment that seems to have been lost in the economies of modern industrial societies as they function today. Since this study is about inflation and unemployment, a

---

*The interwar years were marked by many disturbances, which make a comparison difficult. In some ways they may be considered as a period of transition. During the 1930s there was much unemployment, but almost no inflation. If more expansionary policies had been pursued, there would have been less unemployment but more inflation. The situation would then have had some similarity to that of today.

TABLE 1.2: Variations During Business Cycles, 1872-1907

Prices (minerals)	*Wages*	*Rates of interest*	*Unemployment*
1873 max.	1877 max.	1873 max.	1872 min.
1879 min.	1879 min.	1879 min.	1879 max.
1882 max.	1882 max.	1884 max.	1882 min.
1885 min.	1886 min.	1886 min.	1886 max.
1890 max.	1890 max.	1890 max.	1890 min.
1895 min.	1893 min.	1895 min.	1893 max.
1900 max.	1899 max.	1900 max.	1899 min.
1904 min.	1903 min.	1905 min.	1904 max.
1907 max.	—	1907 max.	1906 min.

Source: Gustav Cassel, *The Theory of Social Economy* (New York: Augustus M. Kelly, 1967), bk. IV.

comparison with the past is particularly interesting as regards the general trends of prices, wages, and unemployment.

As far as prices are concerned, it can be seen from Figure 1.1 that they showed a downward trend from about 1875-80 until about 1895, then moved upward until 1910-14, when the level was more or less the same as in 1875-80.

As for wages, a few figures from the study by Cassel can serve as an illustration of the nature of their movements.[4]

Shipbuilding and Mechanical Engineering, U.K. (1900 = 100)	
1850	68
1854	76
1860	73
1866	79
1867	77
1877	88
1879	83
1882	88
1886	84
1890	93
1893	100
1963	99

Coal Mining Germany, DM Per Shift	
1872	4.50
1873	5.00
1879	2.55
1883	3.15
1886	2.92
1891	4.08
1900	5.16
1902	4.57
1907	5.98
1909	5.33

It will be seen that wages moved up and down, especially in the case of coal mining in Germany. These figures do not show any clear trend. In the British shipbuilding and mechanical engineering industries, there was an average increase of about 0.75 percent per year during the period covered by the figures. During this long period, however, labor productivity increased at least as much as wages. The real price of labor, therefore, hardly increased.

As far as unemployment is concerned, Cassel shows the average percentages for five years of minimum and five years of maximum for the period from 1872 to 1908. They cover five different sectors of British industry and are shown below.[5]

	Min.	*Max.*
Shipbuilding, engineering	2.4	12.2
Construction	3.0	7.7
Wood and furniture	2.9	6.4
Printing, bookbinding	2.9	4.2
Other branches	1.1	3.4

It will be seen that the differences between the average minimums and the average maximums are considerable, especially for the first two branches, which are typical investment goods industries. They are much smaller for the last two groups, which are typical consumer goods industries. Wood and furniture is somewhere in between. It is important to note that the figures show no clear trend for the period as a whole.

This brief review of the period from about 1870 to the years just before World War I shows a picture that is very different from that of the 1960s and 1970s. Prices of both products and labor moved up and down, and there was no clear trend for the period as a whole. The same was true of unemployment.

It is, therefore, a new feature of the economies of modern industrial societies that fairly high rates of both inflation and unemployment seem to have become persistent evils. The structures of these societies have changed drastically since about 1870. Technically, economically, and politically they represent systems that are very different from those of 1870 and even from those of 1914.

The systems of the former period were not perfect—far from it. A substantial part of the population lived in poverty, and those who became unemployed were in a truly bad situation. But while much progress has been made since then, the systems have at the same time become less self-adjusting. The question is, therefore, what changes in the modern societies have led to this loss of self-adjustment. That is the subject of the next chapter.

NOTES

1. J. M. Keynes, *The General Theory of Employment, Interest and Money* (London: MacMillan & Co., 1936).
2. OECD, *Economic Outlook* 25 (July 1979): 10.
3. Gustav Cassel, *The Theory of Social Economy* (New York: Augustus M. Kelly, 1967), bk. IV.
4. Ibid., pp. 606, 608.
5. Ibid., p. 576.

2

ORGANIZATION IN THE MODERN SOCIETY

If we look for the changes in society that have made some adjustment processes less flexible than they were in former times, we will find that they are rather heterogeneous. Nevertheless, one feature is characteristic of nearly all of them: they can be considered as aspects of the growing role of organization in modern societies.

The markets of products (goods and services), labor, and capital have become more organized. At the same time, a growing public sector has organized the steadily growing systems of education, health services, social security schemes, protection of the environment, and so on. And to an increasing extent, both private and public systems of organization have been extended beyond the national borders. Organization is becoming international in many fields.

First we shall look at the organization of the various markets of which a modern economy is composed, and then consider the public sector. There are three categories of markets: the markets for products (goods and services), and the markets for the two factors of production: labor and capital. The factors of production can, of course, be grouped in various ways, and in some respects it is an oversimplification to talk about only two factors of production.

In a previous book I distinguished four factors of production: land, labor, capital, and knowledge.[1] By land is understood both argicultural land and other natural resources, such as minerals, fish in the seas, and so on. By knowledge is understood technical, commercial, financial, administrative, and other knowledge, which has been of increasing importance to the development of production and of society in general.

However, as regards the organization of markets, land will usually be combined with capital, and knowledge will be combined with labor or with capital. A farm or factory is a piece of land on which some capital has been invested, such as buildings and cattle and/or machinery. Modern machinery is capital in which much technical knowledge has been invested, and the value of, for example, the work done by an engineer has been enhanced by the knowledge he has acquired. In some cases land or knowledge can be sold separately—for instance, if it is a piece of virgin forest or a patent. In the markets these two items are, however, treated as if they were capital.

Therefore unless otherwise indicated, the factors of production will in this book be considered as consisting of two categories, labor and capital.

PRODUCT MARKETS

In former times the markets for goods and services were, as a general rule, unorganized. There were many buyers and sellers, and none of them had any appreciable influence on the development of the market or the prevailing prices. If a farmer had wheat for sale, he was bound to accept the existing market price, which nobody had actually fixed but was the result of the interplay of the offers made by and the demands from a large number of actors competing without any leader.

This system is known as free or perfect competition. Though there have been markets where a large buyer or seller could exert some influence, at least part of the time, markets in general have been rather close to this type of competition.

When prices moved up and down as described in Chapter 1, it was exactly because no seller was strong enough to prevent them from falling and no buyer was strong enough to prevent them from rising. This is what has changed, and the main reason is that drastic technical development has created productive units very different from those that were common in the 19th century.

The up-to-date methods of production have to an increasing extent required fairly large investments in buildings and machinery, and often in research and development and in building up a sales organization as well.

This has had two consequences. One is that it has favored the development of large enterprises. In 1972 the four largest enterprises in the United States accounted for more than half of the total sales in 127 out of 429 industries. In 1970, the same was true in Sweden in 17 out of 21 industries.[2] It is obviously easier to dominate the market in a small country than in a large one.

The other consequence of the need to invest so much is that there are large fixed costs that must be paid whether sales are good or bad. Thus, there is a risk that makes it important for firms to defend their position in the market. Therefore, we have seen a tendency for firms to give their products a special image, perhaps protected by a trademark, and to make the products known by advertising them. The firm thus gets a market of its own, in a way.

This, as well as the high costs of investment, makes it difficult to establish new firms in line of production, and newcomers to the market may meet with keen price competition until they succumb and are taken over by an existing firm.

In fact, mergers of firms have played a great role in the postwar period, which is one of the reasons why so many branches of trade are dominated by a few large firms. The market power of these firms can be enhanced through the formation of cartels or through informal understandings, the aim of which is to reach agreements on prices or to share the market.

In the next chapter there will be a discussion of how this market power contributes to the tendency of prices to go on rising even in periods of weakening demand. There is, however, one aspect of this problem that should be considered first because it has to do with the nature of the organization of the markets.

Why has this organization strengthened the position of the sellers so much? Why has there not been any countervailing power that could strengthen the position of the buyers to the same extent? The answer is that some efforts in this direction have been made. In many countries there are cooperative societies organized by consumers. These societies have established retail stores, and sometimes also factories in which they produce goods to be distributed through the stores. On the whole, though, the influence of the cooperative societies has been limited.

The main reason for that is no doubt that by the nature of things they were latecomers. Throughout history, those who have organized production in one branch of trade after another have been people who have specialized in the production of something for sale. This is how a number of activities have been removed from the subsistence farms. Spinning, weaving, brick burning, the making of tools, and similar activities became the tasks of specialists, and through the centuries that followed, innovation and the establishment of organization remained in the hands of specialists. Only a specialist could invent the automobile. This could not have been done by a consumer movement.

That is why somebody who has set up an organization based on expert knowledge is in such a strong position. There is only one thing that can create an equally strong countervailing power: the ownership of scarce natural resources needed by the people who run the organizations.

The above is clearly demonstrated by Anthony Sampson in his analysis of the development of the oil industry.[3] He shows how the seven largest oil companies gradually came to dominate the oil market, until the major oil-producing countries, through their own organization, OPEC, became strong enough to take over the price fixing. This, however, meant only that the sellers of this primary product became stronger than those who represented the next steps in the production and distribution. The power was still in the hands of sellers.

It is possible that something similar may happen as far as other primary products are concerned. It remains a general fact that market power on the part of sellers has become a dominant feature of modern societies. This organization of enterprises has gradually transcended national boundaries. Multinational corporations have become an important element in all modern societies, and many such firms also have subsidiaries in less-developed countries.

This is a natural consequence of the technical development that has generally favored the creation of large enterprises. The more countries are included in productions, the better investment in research and development is utilized. Also, modern means of transport and communication have facilitated the administration of corporations that have subsidiaries in many countries.

Multinational corporations have made important contributions to the spread of technology and experience of business administration. From the point of view of organization, multinational corporations have the advantage that to a large extent they can concentrate their activities in countries where, for instance, the level of wages or the laws regarding taxation and price controls are favorable.

This has to do with the problems of both inflation and unemployment. Often the production of finished goods is spread over three, four, or five countries, and none of these countries has any possibility of controlling the profits in a satisfactory way. Transfer pricing of sales from one subsidiary to another has, therefore, become a problem for the authorities of the countries concerned. More will be said about this in the following chapters.

Employment can be influenced if a multinational corporation decides to remove production to countries where conditions are considered better than in the countries where the production has formerly taken place.

Thus, internationalization of business has created new problems for the authorities in the countries concerned.

LABOR MARKETS

One of the results of the development of industry was the creation of a working class. During the early phases of industrialism, the situation of the working class was bad in several countries. It is, therefore, no wonder that efforts were made to organize the workers, and the gradual widening of democracy in the relevant political systems favored this development.

Labor unions have become an important factor in all modern societies, and their role in the fixing of wages and of rules concerning the conditions of work has become more and more important. A countervailing force has been created in the form of employers' associations, and wages are now, to a large extent, fixed after collective bargaining between the organizations representing wage earners and enterprises.

It should be added that in most modern societies, the public sector now employs a substantial part of the labor force. In some countries it accounts for about 30 percent of the total number of workers and employees. This means that public authorities are involved in wage fixing and wage negotiations, and a comparison between public and private wages and salaries may therefore become a political problem.

Though the public sector is the largest employer in many countries, for obvious reasons it cannot join the employers' associations. Anything the political authorities do regarding wages, salaries, and working conditions will be judged in political terms, and these actions will in principle be judged as affecting the labor market as a whole, not only the public sector. More will be said about this in the following chapters.

In relations with their own staff, the public authorities usually follow the trends in the private labor market rather closely. Therefore, the policies of the employers' organizations more or less determine the degree of countervailing forces that the labor unions are to face.

From what has been said above about product markets, it follows that many industries are now dominated by large enterprises that have a certain market power. Thus, to a certain extent they can raise their prices without causing very large reductions in sales. This will particularly be the case after a general wage rise, when a large part of the population has more purchasing power.

It will be shown in the next chapter that in a similar way many small firms in subsectors, such as retail trade and many service trades that are not exposed to foreign competition, will be able to raise their prices to a degree that is fairly close to any increase in labor costs.

In branches that are exposed to international competition, this will in most cases not be possible, unless wages increase correspondingly in the most important countries. If this is not the case, such firms will be faced with considerable wage rises. It should also be taken into account that if a breakdown in the wage negotiations leads to a prolonged strike or lockout, such firms run the risk of losing market shares abroad because their foreign competitors can go on producing while they cannot.

For these various reasons, opposition to wage increases will often be weaker than one might expect. It should be added that general wage negotiations are followed with great interest by the public in modern societies; and, wage earners being the great majority of the population, there will often be psychological pressure on the employers, especially if there are some low-wage groups for whom improvements are requested. Labor unions have, therefore, often been in a relatively strong position, and wages have often increased more than the productivity of labor.

The unit labor costs in the manufacturing industry in the seven largest OECD member countries have shown the following annual increases:[4]

Year(s)	*Percent*
1966-76	5.8
1977	6.8
1978	6.25
1979	6.25

When the political authorities have been involved in wage negotiations, other policy issues, such as taxation and social security, have sometimes been brought up in the discussions. In this way the bargaining parties—the labor unions in particular—have acquired influence of a more general political nature.

A number of international labor organizations have been created. In cases of conflicts involving the subsidiaries of a multinational corporation in one country, strikes or the threats of strikes against subsidiaries of the same corporation in other countries have sometimes been used to put pressure on the corporation as a whole.

It was to be expected that as the business sector was becoming more and more internationalized, the same would happen to labor. So far, however, the results have been limited. Vis-à-vis the multinational corporations, labor unions are in the same situation as the national authorities. It is very difficult to get a clear picture of the real situation of a union working in many countries. Also, there is a limit to the sacrifices that workers in one country are prepared to make in order to support their colleagues in other countries.[5]

In conclusion, it may be said that market power has become an important factor in the labor markets of modern societies. As in product markets, those who sell labor have been strong in their relations with those who buy. This is not only because in democratic societies wage earners are the greater part of the population. It is also because the resistance of the business sector has often been limited. Firms that have market power in the product markets can make concessions in the labor market more easily than others; and if it leads to inflation, those who gain from that will, on the whole, be the enterprises, because the real value of their debts will decrease.

CAPITAL MARKETS

What we call capital markets are in fact markets in financial capital, that is, money or liquidity available in banks and similar institutions for those who want to borrow. Real capital, created by investment, is very different. It consists of buildings, ships, machinery, and other material means of production. These objects are traded in the product markets, but investment is to a large extent financed by borrowing, or the issuing of stocks, in the capital markets. Also, consumption is sometimes partly financed in that way; and, in a general way, financing is required where consumption plus investment exceeds production.

It does not take real resources to create financial capital. The opening of an account in a central bank is sufficient. In addition, there is a credit multiplier in private banking. Increased lending from the banking system will create means for new deposits, which again permits new lending, as long as the relation between cash and outstanding credits is reasonable.

What follows should be read with these facts in mind, because if the capital markets function in such a way that ample liquidity is created, this does not necessarily mean that it will be easy to obtain a rapid increase in real resources for consumption and investment.

In the postwar period there has been a remarkable extension of the organization of capital markets. This has taken place at three levels: in private banking, in the monetary systems of national economies, and through the creation of new international organizations.

In private banking, as in the business sector in general, concentration has become a very important factor. There are now fewer, but often much larger, banks than before World War II. And, as happened in industry, the larger units have extended their activities beyond national borders. Both the lending and the receiving of deposits have taken place across these borders, and some banks have become multinational by establishing subsidiaries in several countries.

More interesting is the fact that some banks have increasingly been operating in currencies other than that of their home country, granting loans and receiving deposits in U.S. dollars and, to some extent, in German, Swiss, Japanese, and other currencies. The bond market has been internationalized in a similar way.

As in the case of multinational corporations, this has opened possibilities of operating in ways that are less influenced by national monetary restrictions than are the ordinary national capital markets. It has been discussed whether this so-called Eurocurrency market has contributed in any important way to the increase in international liquidity through the credit multiplier referred to above. According to a study by Helmut Mayer, this has, on the whole, occurred on a modest scale.[6] But internationally the Eurocurrency system has redistributed the expansionary effects of the U.S. capital outflows. Furthermore, the Eurocurrency system "may tend to blunt the effectiveness of certain domestic monetary policy instruments."[7]

All in all, the extended internationalization of the private banking system and its operations has facilitated capital flows to countries that otherwise would have difficulty borrowing. As will be shown in Chapter 5, this has facilitated the industrial expansion of some less-developed countries and the removal of some labor-intensive activities from the West to these countries.

At the same time, it has weakened the possibility of national monetary authorities' steering the capital flows in which they are interested. As was the case with transactions of multinational enterprises in general, capital transactions also are attracted by countries that have more liberal laws.

For the national authorities an important change took place when the monetary systems were detached from gold. There is no longer any self-adjusting factor—the national gold stock that used to move up and down as the balance of payments became positive or negative. Therefore, monetary policy has become an important political issue. Should it be expansionary or contractionary?

Often, governments and central banks have been faced with a dilemma in this respect. If the product and labor markets are pressing prices and wages upward, the amount of money available for circulation must be increased in order to finance the transactions occurring. If not, a reduction of production and employment will take place. The authorities will, therefore, be under pressure to allow a monetary expansion.

But if they do so, the inflation created by the functioning of the product and labor markets may be reinforced. By increasing total demand, the authorities may further increase the deterioration of the balance of payments, which may have resulted from the price rises if the latter have exceeded those of the other major countries.

Faced with this dilemma, governments will find it easier to pursue expansionary monetary policies than it was in former times, even if it means that a balance-of-payments deficit will have to be financed by borrowing abroad. The development of the private banking system described above should facilitate such borrowing. The same is true of international financial institutions, which will be discussed below.

To this must be added that during the postwar period, a number of countries have established bilateral agreements, called swap arrangements, allowing one country to draw on another's central bank and vice versa. It is important to note that the effects of such a bilateral agreement are not always limited to the two countries directly involved. If country A draws the currency of country B, this currency can be sold in the international markets and thus be exchanged for other currencies. Like the expansion of the private banking system, such arrangements tend to facilitate capital flows between countries. They also make it easier for a country to run a balance-of-payments deficit.

A special mention should be made of the United States because the U.S. dollar has been widely used in international transactions. Therefore, it has also been widely accepted as part of the official foreign-exchange reserves of other countries. During 1971-78 the total increase in these reserves, which consists of official claims on countries, was distributed as shown below.[8]

	Billion SDRs
Claims on the United States	121.1
Claims on other countries	13.0

Apart from these official claims, there are also large holdings of U.S. dollars in the hands of private banks and enterprises in many countries.

This has made it particularly easy for the United States to have a balance-of-payments deficit, to a large extent consisting of capital exports to other countries. As already indicated, this capital outflow has had an expansionary effect that has been spread to many countries by the Eurocurrency system.

Of the new international financial institutions created during the postwar period, the International Monetary Fund (IMF) is particularly important, since countries can draw foreign currencies from it when they have balance-of-payments deficits. This is subject to certain rules, and in some cases the IMF has made it a condition that cautious fiscal and monetary policies are pursued. Nevertheless, besides those already mentioned, it represents one more possibility of financing deficits. It should be noted that in addition to gold and the national currencies that the member countries have deposited with the IMF as its working capital, the IMF has also started issuing its own currency, the special drawing rights (SDRs), which may become of increasing importance in the future.

Other important institutions from the postwar period are the World Bank and a number of regional development banks, which are now major instruments for the moving of capital to less-developed countries. This capital is partly paid in by member countries and partly borrowed in the international capital markets. The expansion of the capital markets already referred to has therefore facilitated this beneficial financing of the development of poor societies. It may, however, also have acted as a lever for market power and for national policies, which have contributed to the widespread inflation that has increasingly characterized the postwar period.

It seems a paradox that the growing organization of markets appears to have made product and labor markets tighter, strengthening the position of those who have something to sell, while it has also made capital markets easier, strengthening the position of those who have to borrow.

No doubt, this has to do with the fact that the capital market is not a market in real resources, since liquidity can be created simply by certain decisions or financial transactions being made. In the product and labor markets, on the other hand, real resources are traded, the supply of them not being unlimited. Therefore, those who command this supply can obtain market power through appropriate forms of organization.

The results of these apparently opposite tendencies do, however, support one another to a large extent. The market power of products and labor tends to press prices and wages upward. Therefore, transactions require on increasing amount of money, and the expansionary tendencies in the capital markets make more money or liquidity available, thus facilitating the upward movement.

How these combined new forces have contributed to the present process of inflation will be discussed in the next chapter. Before that we shall consider the public sector, which has become such an important factor in all modern economies.

THE PUBLIC SECTOR

The public sector has been growing fast in all modern societies since World War II. As a percentage of gross domestic product (GDP), the total public expenditure has developed as shown below for 18 OECD member countries and for OECD as a whole:[9]

	1955-57	*1967-69*	*1974-76*
Lowest percentage	15	19	24
Highest percentage	34	42.5	54
OECD average	23.5	34.5	41.5

The increase has been particularly fast as regards welfare expenditure—education, health, and income maintenance schemes such as pensions, child allowances, and unemployment benefits. This has contributed to a dampening of business cycles because incomes are maintained more than in former times during the downward phase of the cycle. Indirectly the increase may, however, also have supported inflationary tendencies because it has counteracted the tendency for prices and wages to fall during that phase, as described in Chapter 1.

Since public expenditure now forms such a large part of the national economies, fiscal policy has become an important subject for political discussions. Total demand can be increased by public expenditure being raised or by taxes being lowered. It can be reduced by measures being taken in the opposite direction. In these ways employment can be influenced, but changes in fiscal policy are also likely to influence the rate of inflation and the balance of payments.

This responsibility for the economy as a whole, bestowed on the political authorities, is added to the one regarding monetary policy that was described in the previous section. Altogether, it means that the way the public sector is managed has a considerable influence on the markets for products, labor, and capital.

At the same time there has been an increasing inclination on the part of public authorities to interfere directly in the functioning of these markets.

As regards product markets, there has been a tendency in many countries to support agriculture by protection, export subsidies, or measures aiming at guaranteeing minimum prices. In these ways efforts are made to give agriculture a market power similar to the one created in industry by concentration and cartels. Though the average size of farms is increasing, there are still far too many producers in the agricultural markets for them to get this market power through their own efforts.

On the other hand, price control—or, more generally, what is called competition policy—is used to limit the effects of market power in the business sector. This has counteracted inflationary tendencies. It is difficult to form an opinion of the efficacy of these policies, which vary from country to country. An obvious weakness is that the transfer pricing of multinational corporations cannot be controlled efficiently by any single country. More will be said about this important problem in Chapter 6.

As far as labor markets are concerned, the market power of the unions has been strengthened by the various national schemes of unemployment compensation, which are now to a large extent financed by the public sector. In collective bargaining, during which wages are fixed, the bargaining parties can now feel more or less free of responsibility for the contribution to both inflation and unemployment that may be one of the results of the agreement they are making. Therefore, these agreements are among the features of modern economies that deserve reconsideration. This will, therefore, also be one of the issues to be discussed in Chapter 6.

During the 1960s and 1970s the much more general question of a wage policy has been the subject of lively discussions in many countries. Since wages are substantially more than half the sum of incomes in all modern societies, the fixing of wages is of extreme importance in the efforts to limit inflation. At the same time, the relations between labor costs and the prices of the goods to be produced can decide the level of production and employment. Therefore, in a number of cases governments have been involved in wage negotiations. This is, however, an extremely delicate problem, since wage earners are the great majority of the population in modern societies, and some of them have low incomes. More about this question will be said in the following chapters.

To sum up the reasoning of this chapter, it is important to underline the fact that decision making has become a factor having an influence that was inconceivable in the societies of the 19th century. In the old, relatively unorganized markets, no buyer or seller could make decisions that influenced prices in any perceptible way. The reaction of the central banks to changes in the gold stock was nearly automatic, and governments and parliaments interfered only modestly with the working of the economy. This was the age of laissez-faire.

Now, decisions made by the management of a large multinational corporation can have an appreciable influence on prices and employment in several countries. The decisions made during collective bargaining can greatly influence both the rate of inflation and the level of employment. And the public authorities make decisions concerning taxes, social security, education, and monetary policy that may change the working of the economy in a number of ways. Therefore, those who make these decisions have a degree of power unheard of in former times. The fact that we now have persistent inflation and unemployment seems to indicate that the decision making does not function in a harmonious way at the present stage of the continuous development that all societies undergo.

It is probably fair to say that the greatest weakness of the present system of decision making is that decisions are uncoordinated to a very large extent. Each decision maker has a responsibility that is defined by his or her particular position. The decision maker must think of the future of the firm, or try to foresee the reaction of the members of the labor union to a certain decision concerning wages. If the decision maker is a member of the government, thought must be given to the effects of many different decisions on the level of employment, on the rate of inflation, and on the balance of payments. And can there be no thought about the next election?

The art of decision making can be improved if an analysis of the system shows that, carefully considered, the real interests of the various groups in society are less conflicting than they appear to be in many political discussions. That will be the subject of Chapter 6.

NOTES

1. Thorkil Kristensen, *Development in Rich and Poor Countries* (New York: Praeger, 1974), pp. 6-9.
2. OECD, *Concentration and Competition Policy* (Paris: OECD, 1979), Tables 2.11, 2.13.
3. Anthony Sampson, *The Seven Sisters* (New York: Bantam Books, 1979).
4. OECD, *Economic Outlook* 24 (Dec. 1978): Table 22.
5. See Christopher Tugendhat, *The Multinationals* (Harmondsworth: Penguin Books, 1977), Ch. 13.
6. Helmut Mayer, *Credit and Liquidity Creation in the International Banking Sector* (Basel: Bank for International Settlements, 1979), esp. p. 53.
7. Ibid., p. 65.
8. International Monetary Fund, *Annual Report 1979* (Washington D.C.: IMF, 1979), Table 17.
9. *OECD Observer* no. 92 (May 1978): 8.

3 INFLATION

In principle, prices may rise for two different reasons. They can be pulled upward because demand in the economy is increasing. This is usually called demand-pull inflation. Or they can be pushed upward because those who sell labor, raw materials, intermediary products, and other factors have sufficient market power to enforce such rises. This is usually called cost-push inflation.

In some cases the prices of the end products sold in the market may be pushed upward simply because those who sell them have sufficient market power. This may happen even if costs have not been pushed upward first. The oil price rises of the 1970s were not a result of higher costs of production in the OPEC member countries. Oil prices were raised because these countries had discovered that they had very strong market power.

For the above reason, I shall use the terms "demand-pull inflation" and "price/cost-push inflation." In the latter case, prices are raised because of the market power possessed by those who sell the products or some of the means of production needed to produce them.

In the first years after World War II, it was widely believed that excess demand could pull prices and wages upward only when there was nearly full employment and, in a more general way, nearly full utilization of the productive capacity. If this was not the case, increased demand would mainly lead to an increase in production, and thus to a higher level of employment. This situation has changed because of the increased market organization described in Chapter 2. Now prices and wages can be raised even if there is considerable idle capacity and unemployment.

It is not always easy to distinguish between demand-pull inflation and price/cost-push inflation. If, in a society with idle capacity and unemployment, demand is increased by expansionary fiscal policies, production and employment will also be increased, though not much, as prices and wages are raised so that less can be bought for the larger amount of income. The higher level of demand means that producers and labor unions can get more out of their market power, because the additional demand gives them a larger field in which to apply this power.

In such a case there is no clear-cut distinction between demand-pull and price/cost-push inflation. Prices and wages increase, partly because more demand has been created, but also partly because the existing market power enables firms and unions to charge higher prices and to raise wages. Thus, the effect on the level of production and employment is limited.

The present combination of inflation and unemployment seems to indicate that it is exactly situations like the one described above that complicate the tasks of policy makers today. It is still important to see to it that the level of total demand is neither too high nor too low, but the efficacy of demand management has been reduced by the changed ways in which the mechanisms of product and labor markets function. An analysis of the present inflation problem must start with a look at these mechanisms.

In their effects on inflation, the market systems of products and labor are so closely intertwined that we probably understand them best if we treat them as one combined, complex system of markets. This has to do with the important fact that in the product markets some producers have much more market power than others, but they compete for labor in the same labor market. It should become clear from the analysis of this and the following chapter that up to a point, both the inflation and the unemployment of the present period can be explained by this combination of market conditions.

COMPETING AND SHELTERED SECTORS

Between 1960 and 1968, OECD export prices rose at an annual rate of 0.75 percent, compared with 3.25 percent for domestic prices.[1] This shows that the parts of the product markets that were exposed to foreign competition were able to raise prices much less than the parts that were sheltered from such competition.

This difference between two sectors of the economy has been dealt with in more detail as far as Sweden is concerned in a valuable study that also treats the labor market in relation to the two sectors.[2] The study uses the terms C (competing) and S (sheltered) for the two sectors; the main results are summarized in Table 11.3 of the book.

TABLE 3.1: Prices, Productivity, and Wages; Selected Countries and Years (annual increases, percent)

	Prices		*Productivity*		*Value Added**		*Wages*	
Sweden	*C*	*S*	*C*	*S*	*C*	*S*	*C*	*S*
1952-60	0.9	3.7	4.2	2.2	5.1	6.0	6.5	6.5
1960-68	1.2	4.7	8.2	3.8	9.5	8.7	10.2	9.5
Other countries								
1970-75								
Austria	5.1	7.0	5.9	2.2	11.3	9.4	13.2	12.4
Belgium	5.4	9.8	5.1	2.3	10.8	12.3	16.7	16.0
Netherlands	7.0	15.2	5.9	2.0	13.3	17.5	15.5	14.9
France	7.8	9.7	4.4	2.9	12.5	12.9	14.6	14.5
United Kingdom	13.0	15.2	2.1	0.5	15.3	15.8	17.0	18.1
United States	8.4	6.2	2.0	0.4	10.6	6.6	7.6	8.2

*Price of products minus cost price of raw materials.

Sources: International Labour Organization, *Yearbook of Labour Statistics* (Geneva: International Labour Organization, 1976), various tables; OECD, *National Accounts of OECD Countries* (1960-77), various tables.

In Table 3.1, I have compared these figures for Sweden for the periods 1952-60 and 1960-68 with more recent figures for other countries. The table shows the annual percent increases, and I have calculated the increase in the value added by multiplying the price increase by the productivity increase. In the Swedish study the latter is defined as the increase in product per man-hour and can therefore be compared with the increase in hourly wages.

This table shows some regularities that reflect the nature of the two sectors. First, prices have increased substantially more in the sheltered sector than in the competing one, with two exceptions. In the United Kingdom the difference is modest, and in the United States prices in the competing sector have shown the highest rate of increase. This is because the currencies of these two countries, especially the British, were devalued during the period covered by the table. A devaluation means that the prices of imported and exported goods increase, measured in the national currency; therefore, prices can be raised in the sector that is exporting or competing with imports.

On the other hand, in the Netherlands prices in the competing sector have increased very much less than those in the sheltered one. This is because the Dutch currency was revalued during the period in question. The effect of a revaluation on the prices in foreign trade is the opposite of that of a devaluation.

Second, the increase in wages has been approximately the same in the two sectors. This is because they compete for labor in the same national labor market. It would not for any length of time be possible for one of the sectors to keep its workers at wages that were increasing substantially less than those prevailing in the rest of the labor market.

Third, productivity has increased faster in the competing sector than in the sheltered one. This has been necessary because the competing sector has had to accept much lower price increases than the other sector, while its labor costs have risen at roughly the same rates as those of the sector whose prices were increasing more.

That is, the competing sector has been forced to rationalize production much more than the other sector. As a general rule this rationalization has consisted in replacing expensive labor with capital through mechanization. When the price of labor increases compared with the prices of the goods produced, there is a natural tendency to produce these goods with a reduced input of labor. This has been particularly the case in the competing sector.

Fourth, as a general rule wages have increased more than the value added. Thus, there must have been a general tendency to save labor, though it has been less pronounced in the sheltered sector than in the competing one. It will be shown in the next chapter that this is one of the causes of the high rates of unemployment that exist in 1980.

Fifth, to revert to the question of inflation, it may be noted that the table seems to show that market power has had an inflationary effect in two parts of the system. In the sheltered sector it has had an inflationary effect because competition in this sector has been much more limited than in the competing one. Therefore, prices could be raised more. In the competing sector the period considered was characterized by general tariff reductions agreed upon in General Agreement on Tariffs and Trade (GATT), and by the almost complete abolition of tariffs on industrial goods moving between the member countries of the Common Market (EEC) and European Free Trade Area (EFTA). Therefore, foreign trade is closer to free competition than it was at the beginning of the period covered by the table. This has prevented a substantial price rise.

The other part of the system in which market power has had an inflationary effect is the labor market. Not only have wages increased more than prices, especially in the competing sector, but in particular they have increased more than labor productivity. Thus, unit labor costs have been rising and part of the increase in the value added is due to these increases in the real price of labor.

This analysis, then, seems to confirm the impression that market power played an important role in the process of inflation during the period covered by the table. Prices rose considerably more in the part of the economies where competition was weak than in the part where it was strong. On the whole, demand conditions must have been the same in the two sectors. It is therefore reasonable to conclude that the new type of persistent inflation has primarily been of the price/cost-push variety.

This also seems to be in conformity with the picture that the table gives of the labor market. The unions apparently have had the upper hand in their relations with employers. Therefore, they have been able to push wages upward to such an extent that workers have gotten a slightly increasing part of the value added resulting from the production processes.

CONCENTRATION AND MARKET POWER

The two-sector model discussed above represents an oversimplification. It probably shows a realistic picture of the sheltered sector. Retail trade, handicrafts, and services, like those of lawyers, doctors, dentists, and hairdressers, are not exposed to foreign competition.

And though supermarkets are now competing with the traditional retail trade, the fact that there is a need to have shops in all parts of a town and in many villages limits the degree of competition. This also means that when wages are raised, prices in the sheltered sector can be raised as a direct consequence of the wage increase. As a general rule that is not the case in the sector exposed to foreign competition.

It is in this competing sector that the model represents an oversimplification. In fact, the degree of competition varies greatly within this sector. The main reason for this is that in some branches production is highly concentrated, while in others the degree of concentration is much lower. If a few firms dominate the national market of a large country, they are often in a strong position even if they have to compete with imports. It must be remembered that when a large industrial firm has succeeded in giving its products a special image, different from those of competing products, this makes competition somewhat less severe. Often there will be an informal understanding among some of the major firms in the branch that limits competition. Much depends, therefore, on the degree of competition, as indicated in Chapter 2.

The OECD report *Concentration and Competition Policy* states in its conclusions:

> The central chapters in this report tend to show that concentration is already very high in a number of important (often the same) industries in several countries, and it has been increasing in the recent past, sometimes rapidly, in a significant number of these and of other less concentrated industries. Overall concentration appears to be fairly high and steadily increasing in most countries, if not at a spectacularly high rate.[3]

The question now is to what extent this concentration has strengthened the market power of enterprises so that their price-fixing can have contributed to the inflation of recent decades. This problem has been dealt with in various studies. Some of them are quoted in the OECD report just mentioned, and others are summarized by Dennis Swann. He concludes: "The effect of concentration on profitability is well supported by empirical evidence."[4] By profitability he means the price-cost ratio measured as a gross profit margin on sales. As could be expected, on the whole the studies in the field confirm that concentration strengthens market power, but to varying degrees.

One of these studies is of particular interest, since it covers the development of more than 100 American manufacturing industries from 1948 to 1970.[5] The subject of this study is price markups, defined as the selling price of the goods produced, divided by the direct labor and raw material costs.

Firms are divided into three groups on the basis of the degree of market concentration in 1967. In the group described as having high concentration, the four largest firms represented more than 50 percent of total sales. In the medium concentration group the four largest firms accounted for between 25 and 50 percent of the sales, and in the low concentration group they had less than 25 percent.

In all three groups the price markups increased during the period covered by the study, but the more so the higher the degree of concentration. If we put the price markups in 1948 at 100, they had reached the following levels in 1970:

Concentration	*Index*
High	172.03
Medium	135.96
Low	103.83

The fact that markups increased during the period means that the price fixing of the enterprises contributed to inflation. On the whole they gained in strength, and in this respect the differences among the three groups diminished. The low concentration group to some extent caught up with the other two during the 1960s and the medium concentration group came closer to the high concentration group.

The study shows another feature that is of particular interest because it tells something about the ways in which organized markets function. During the 22 years covered by the study, there were five short recessions and four periods of expansion. The average percentage changes of the markups in each recession and in each expansion are shown below.

Concentration	*Recession*	*Expansion*
High	+8.51	+ 4.05
Medium	-2.89	+12.22
Low	-2.43	+ 4.44

Interestingly the high concentration group was able to strengthen its position during the recessions, when demand was weak. In these periods raw material prices may have fallen, and unit labor costs declined during the recession of 1960-61. Therefore, if the high concentration group could maintain its prices and perhaps even raise them slightly during such periods, the price markups were bound to increase.

The other two groups were obviously in a weaker position during the recessions. Their performance was closer to the pattern shown in Chapter 1 for the markets of former times when prices went up and down during the business cycles. However, in this respect, too, they have gradually come closer to the high concentration group. During the last two recessions the percentage changes in their price markups were those shown below.

Concentration	*1960-61*	*1969-70*
Medium	- 1.86	+1.34
Low	+ .82	+2.54

Thus, there seems to have developed a pattern in which all the groups maintain their prices well during a recession. This corresponds well to the description of postwar inflation in Chapter 1, according to which prices continued to rise during 1955-60, when the raw material boom experienced in the Korean War had come to an end, and also during 1977 and 1978, when the real price of oil fell slightly.

What we have examined here is the market power of enterprises. Where there is concentration, they seem increasingly to have become masters of their own price fixing, so that prices continue to rise even during a recession. But to his conclusion quoted above, Swann adds the following sentence: "It may be that the main influence of market power is not that it enhances profitability, but that it inflates costs (and the latter causes profits to be less than they otherwise would be)."[6]

This raises an important question. The markups described above are gross profits—the product prices divided by the direct, variable costs of labor and raw materials. But to determine net profits, one must also count the indirect, fixed costs of capital and of the salaried staff required for maintaining the enterprise and for the development of new products and methods of production. If these overhead costs have increased because production has become more capital-intensive and more sophisticated, net profits may not have increased at all in many enterprises.

It is therefore necessary to examine the cost structures in modern production systems.

COST STRUCTURES

The importance of the structure of costs has been illustrated by Paolo Sylos-Labrini.[7] He has described the distribution of the value

TABLE 3.2: Percentage Distribution of Value Added; Italy and United States, 1951-52 and 1976-77

	Italy		*United States*	
	1951-52	*1976-77*	*1951-52*	*1976-77*
Wages	38.1	43.3	41.1	33.5
Salaries	6.5	18.2	19.4	29.8
Capital consumption	5.6	10.5	6.3	11.3
Other overhead	19.8	16.4	9.2	12.0
Profit	30.0	11.6	24.0	13.4
	100.0	100.0	100.0	100.0

Source: Paolo Sylos-Labrini, "Prices and Income Distribution in Manufacturing Industry," *Journal of Post-Keynesian Economics* 2, no. 1 (1979): 12.

added in the manufacturing industry in Italy and the United States, as shown in Table 3.2. Costs of raw materials are not included—only what is added to the value of these materials when they have been transformed by the industry and sold as products.

There has been a spectacular increase in fixed costs—salaries and capital consumption (depreciation)—and at the same time profits have been reduced. The table covers only two countries, but the trends it indicates are of a general nature. In modern societies production has become more sophisticated and more capital-intensive, and there has also been a general tendency for profits to decline.

This leads to two conclusions that seem to have general validity regarding the development of modern economies. One is that the increasing price markups give an incomplete picture of the economic situation of enterprises. The price markups show the gross profits—sales revenue minus the direct, variable costs of labor and raw materials. In order to find the net profits, one must also deduct the fixed labor costs—salaries—and other overhead, both of which have been increasing quickly.

The other conclusion to be drawn is that because of these large fixed costs, a modern enterprise is vulnerable. The fixed costs must be covered whether a factory is producing or not, whether production is small or large, and whether prices are low or high.

This is why the business sector has been relatively weak in its negotiations with labor unions. It is of great importance that the factories be kept running. If they have to close down during a strike or lockout, nothing is earned to cover the overhead, and in addition there is a risk that competitors in other countries may increase their shares of the market at the closed factories' expense.

It should also be remembered that ordinary wages for factory work are now a less dominant cost factor than they were a few decades ago, especially in highly industrialized countries like the United States. In Table 3.2 they represent only 33.5 percent of the value added in the United States for 1976-77. If raw materials had been added, the percentage would have been even lower compared with the value of sales.

Partly for that reason, and partly because enterprises with market power are able to shift a sometimes considerable part of the wage increases on to the consumers through higher prices, such enterprises will often accept wage increases more readily than one would expect.

Salaries are also to a large extent subject to collective bargaining in several countries, but as far as the higher ranks of the professional staff are concerned, salaried persons are much closer to management and to the enterprise as such than are the workers in the factory. Therefore, it is probably fair to say that ordinary wages form part of the price calculations of an enterprise much more directly than do salaries. The additional, variable costs per unit produced are the extra expenditures on raw materials, energy, and wages. The salaried staff does not vary with the size of the production in the same way.

This means that there is much uncertainty in price calculations in a modern enterprise. What is certain is the direct, variable costs of raw materials, energy, and wages per unit produced. But how much should be added as a contribution to the overhead costs of the enterprise? And how should these overhead costs be distributed among the various products manufactured in the factory?

It can be seen from Table 3.1 that as a general rule wages have increased more than value added. This means that they represent an increasing share of the results of industrial production. Though the line of division between wages and salaries may not always be clear, it seems fair to conclude that workers (in the general sense of the word) have earned an increasing part of the results of industry. This has happened in a period when the progress of industry has to a large extent been due to an input of salaried professional staff and of capital that increased much faster than the input of ordinary labor on the factory floor.

This means that in a period when many enterprises have earned more because of increasing market power, a large part of these earnings has been transferred to wage earners through higher wages. Roughly speaking, there are three reasons why this has happened. One is the vulnerability of modern enterprises discussed in this section. The other two have to do with important, specific features of the functioning of modern societies. They will be considered separately in the next two subsections.

RESEARCH AND DEVELOPMENT

During the postwar period, production has increased, on the whole, faster than during the decades before World War II. In everyday language this fact is usually referred to as a rapid increase in productivity. But productivity of what?

In economic reports one often reads that there has been an annual increase in labor productivity of, for example, 2 or 3 percent. In other reports one may read that the productivity of land has increased because more grain can be grown per hectare. In fact, both of these expressions are oversimplifications. Production is the combined result of various factors of production working together, and none of these factors can make the contribution it is said to make without being combined with other factors.

If more can be grown on a certain piece of land, it is not because the land has become better. It is because more fertilizer has been added and because of the results of new research, often in more than one branch of science. If a worker can produce more per hour, it will seldom be because of working harder. It is because work is being combined with better machinery or with other results of ongoing efforts to improve methods of production.

In my book *Development in Rich and Poor Countries* I have distinguished four factors of production: land, labor, capital, and knowledge. In most of the present book it has been sufficient to talk about labor and capital, since land and knowledge are usually combined with capital and/or labor in the markets so that it will suffice to talk about the capital and labor markets.

However, in order to understand modern production processes and their influence on income distribution, we will have to examine all four factors. Their roles are described in Chapter 2 of *Development in Rich and Poor Countries*.

Land and labor are the original factors of production. They already existed when man took food from the land in the most primitive ways. Capital and knowledge have been added gradually throughout history. Because these two factors have been added, we get much more out of a certain piece of land and of an hour's work than did our forefathers. In modern language, capital and knowledge in combination have increased the productivity of land and labor.

Capital and knowledge are, therefore, the true factors of development. The main difference between more-developed and less-developed countries is that the former have applied more capital and knowledge to their land and labor than have the latter. Knowledge is the dynamic or active factor of development. Capital is a more passive factor. The origins of the steam engine and the automobile were new ideas—new knowledge—but metal and other materials were needed in order to make useful instruments on the basis of this knowledge.

I mention these facts because what has happened to the economies during the postwar period is, first and foremost, that there has been unusual progress in knowledge; and in order to utilize this new knowledge, much more capital has had to be invested than formerly. This has increased what we usually call land and labor productivity, but it should be obvious from this brief description that things are more complicated than that.

The question now is who pays for this large investment in knowledge and in capital and who benefits from it. To a large extent investment in science, and in the spreading of its results through education, is paid for by the public sector. Therefore, the whole population contributes to it indirectly.

Much research and development is, however, financed by private enterprises. Some of the major multinational corporations have invested large sums in basic and applied science and in the development of new products and improved methods of production. This is one reason why their salaried staff has increased. The results have been new or better products, and sometimes cheaper products. Another part of the results has been improved methods of production, often through techniques that are more labor-saving than those previously used.

Those who benefit from this are, in the first instance, the corporations. They can increase their sales or reduce their direct, variable costs of production. This means that such direct costs have been replaced by indirect, overhead costs, as can be seen from Table 3.2, especially in the United States.

It is, however, in the nature of knowledge that it tends to spread. This fact is of particular importance in our time, when the level of general knowledge is so high. The more general knowledge one has, the easier it is to develop one's understanding in a particular field. Both the Soviet Union and China have been able to develop the nuclear weapons without getting the knowledge from the United States.

In business specific knowledge can be protected through patents, but only for a certain period. Nothing can prevent others from inventing something that can satisfy needs rather close to those served by the patented product.

This brings us to the most decisive question regarding research and development. Who will, in the long run, get the main benefits of this investment? The answer is that the people who will enjoy the greatest advantage will be in two different groups. One is the consumers who get new or better, and perhaps cheaper, products. The progress in the standards of living that has taken place during the postwar period is largely a result of research and development in the widest sense of these terms. The other group is wage earners. The value of their work per hour has increased much faster than in earlier periods, causing real wages to become much higher than before World War II.

The introduction of labor-saving techniques is one of the causes of the present unemployment; this problem will be dealt with in the next chapter. For those who keep their jobs, the advantage of the progress in research and development is obvious. After a while the advantages of these efforts are bound to be transferred to the consumers and the wage earners. The enterprises cannot keep them to themselves for any length of time. The strength of the large corporation lies in its market power and in the organization it has built up, not in the specific secrets it may have discovered, which are bound to leak sooner or later.

Even the advantages of market power will to a large extent be transferred to the wage earners. If a corporation has invested large sums in sophisticated machinery and in research and development, this capital can be utilized only by hiring workers to operate the machinery. This is why the labor unions are in such a strong position. In a way, corporations have to pay twice for their development of labor-saving techniques. First, they must invest large sums in research and development and in expensive machinery, thereby obtaining a certain reduction of the staff. They lose this advantage by having to pay higher wages to the staff remaining on the payroll.

All comparisons in real life are imperfect, but there are some similarities between this development in modern industry in general and the more specific development that has taken place in the oil industry. First, the oil companies have built up a vast organization, obtaining both market power and technical perfection. Then they have had to transfer a large part of the gains to the oil-producing countries because they can utilize their organization only by buying oil from them.

In a similar way modern industry has built up a vast organization, obtaining both market power and technical perfection. Then it has had to transfer a large part of the gains to the labor unions because it can utilize this organization only by buying labor from them. This is why, in Table 3.1, wages increased more than the value added in the countries concerned, and why in Table 3.2 profits declined even though much more capital was invested in the industries concerned.

This analysis of corporations, their market force, and their increasing overhead has brought us back to the labor market and the unions. It will therefore be appropriate to finish this analysis of the market mechanisms by an examination of some newer labor market practices.

LABOR MARKET PRACTICES

In a period when inflation is a persistent feature of the economy, there is a temptation to introduce practices that apparently alleviate some of the effects of inflation for part of the population, while their main effect is in fact to reinforce the inflationary process.

It is a widespread human phenomenon that people have the habit of comparing their own situation with that of other people, usually to find that some others have been treated better than they. This is why relative wage movements have become a subject of lively discussion and often of action taken by a group. If, to take an example, research and development efforts have improved labor productivity in a certain industry, with the result that wages have been raised, this may easily provoke requests for similar improvements for other groups of wage earners. And if, in that way, two or three groups have their hourly earnings raised, other groups may feel encouraged to make similar requests so that the movement tends to spread.

Not infrequently such a request is backed by a strike, sometimes in violation of the existing wage agreement, the argument being that essential conditions have changed since that agreement was signed. Such strikes are sometimes launched against fields of activity that are particularly vulnerable or perhaps are of vital importance to society as a whole.

The question of relative wage movements is probably most important in countries with decentralized collective bargaining because there, wages may be fixed at different times in different parts of the economy. Strikes like the ones mentioned above may, however, also take place in countries where wage negotiations are more centralized. In some countries such actions may be started, at least partly, for political reasons by groups in opposition to the existing society. Whatever the motivations may be, wage increases for specific groups, obtained at various times, tend to make such increases part of an ongoing process. Therefore, they also contribute to the continuance of the process of inflation.

Of a more general nature is the inclination to introduce an element of indexation into the wage system. This can be more or less complete, but in any case it means that general price increases will provoke general wage increases, which are again bound to provoke new general price increases. This is important because wages constitute between 60 and 70 percent of GNP in modern societies, and therefore are the dominant element of the cost structures. Thus, indexation contributes in an important way to the wage/price spiral that has become a feature of many economies. In this way it also contributes to the ongoing inflation.

One of the problems of a simple indexation system is that it does not distinguish between the price changes that are favorable to the country in question and those that are unfavorable. If export prices rise, the country becomes richer. If import prices rise, the country becomes poorer. It is interesting that the oil price rises after 1973 have brought about a series of wage increases in many oil-importing countries, though these countries have become poorer because of the oil price rises. This effect can be modified if it is decided that price changes of certain products will not be included in the price index that is used to regulate wages.

After many years of price and wage increases, the opinion has been expressed that increases are beginning to become an autonomous factor in the system. If it is taken for granted that wages must rise by a certain amount per year because they have done so during recent years, people may stop asking whether this is reasonable, or whether anything should be done about it. In several countries there has been a tendency to accept such a trend because it is considered unavoidable.

The danger of this tendency is that not only does it favor continued inflation, it may also create expectations that could encourage speculation on further price rises and provoke requests for wage increases high enough to anticipate next year's price rises. In this way the process of inflation becomes accelerating. This is a danger that should not be forgotten.

Finally, it should be mentioned that collective bargaining is only part of the process of wage fixing. Local agreements are often made in individual enterprises, and usually the so-called wage drift is, therefore, less controlled than the more general negotiations between the organizations. Such local arrangements often reflect the fact that some enterprises are in a stronger position than others. Those in a strong position can accept wage rises that would make production impossible in other firms.

The trouble is that what was said above about most people's interest in relative wage movements will apply in such cases. If wages rise in a strong enterprise, it may be all right there; but if this increase forces weaker enterprises to accept similar rises in order to keep their workers, it may become dangerous to employment. If this trend spreads, it will act as an extra force that favors inflation. I will return to this problem in Chapter 6.

It is obvious that there will be more wage drift if the general level of demand is high than if it is low. The higher the general level of demand, the more enterprises will find that they can afford to accept increases in wages paid. This means that the level of total demand is one of the factors that determine whether there will be inflation, and how much; during the first part of the postwar period there was an inclination to think that this was virtually the only decisive factor.

That is not so. With the present types of market organization, the mechanisms of the product and labor markets work in ways that have inflationary effects. Therefore, these have been discussed first. It remains, however, to be mentioned that the management of total demand is an important factor. This is discussed below.

DEMAND MANAGEMENT

Efforts by political authorities and central banks to determine or at least influence the level of total demand have become an important policy issue because of two changes in society. First, the growth of the public sector has meant that the size and the nature of public expenditure and of taxation can have substantial influence on prices and on the levels of production and employment. Second, the creation of money has become more and more independent of the quantities of gold available, giving central banks a direct responsibility in this field. Monetary policy has become a subject of serious discussion.

Various combinations of fiscal and monetary policies can thus be used to influence the level of total demand. The ways in which this is done can have various social or cultural consequences; but because of the subject of this book, I shall consider only the aspects of the problems that have to do with inflation and unemployment.

Demand management would have been comparatively easy if the system had worked the way it was widely supposed to work during the first postwar years, at least partly under the influence of Keynes. In a simplified way this reasoning stated that if there was unemployment and unutilized capacity in industry, an increase in demand would stimulate production and employment without noticeably influencing prices. It would therefore reduce unemployment without creating inflation. When full employment had been attained and capacity was fully utilized, a further expansion of demand would pull wages and prices upward because production could not be increased.

If there was inflation (which, according to this theory, implied that there was also full employment), a reduction of demand would counteract that inflation. But when a point had been reached where there was relative price stability with full employment, a further reduction of demand would create unemployment. This meant that there would be an equilibrium at a point of approximately full employment and stable prices. If, starting from that point, demand were increased, there would be inflation. If it were reduced, there would be unemployment. The task of demand management would, therefore, be to aim at being as close as possible to this point of equilibrium.

After the first reconstruction/inflation period, 1945-50 (see Table 1.2) and the Korean War, there was a decade or so when many national economies were not very far from this ideal. There was some price increase and some unemployment, but only after the mid-1960s did the two problems become more serious.

Since then, the rates of inflation and of unemployment have become higher, and since 1973 they have been very high by historical standards. The direct effects of the oil price rises have been rather modest. The quadrupling of oil prices at the end of 1973 made a direct contribution to the rise of prices in the OECD countries of only 1.5 percent.[8] If the actual rates of inflation have been much higher, it is because the market mechanisms have worked in the ways described in the previous section. They have of course, only gradually taken on the forms they now have.

That they now work this way has made demand management much more difficult. It has increasingly been recognized that with the present market mechanisms there are bound to be high rates of inflation and unemployment at the same time, and it has been assumed that there is a relationship between the two. The generally accepted view has been that even when there is a substantial rate of unemployment, an expansion of demand will make wages and prices rise, and the goal of full employment may never be reached.

With the Phillips curve Prof. A. W. H. Phillips tried in 1958 to define this relationship in an article in *Economica*: the lower the rate of unemployment, the higher the rate of inflation, and vice versa. The percentages he found were substantially lower than those experienced in recent years, but it is still a widely held view that there is an inverse relationship between the two rates.

This naturally creates a serious dilemma for the political authorities. If they pursue an expansionary fiscal and/or monetary policy, there will, at least for a while, be less unemployment, but there will be more inflation. If they choose a contractionary policy, there may be less inflation, but there will be more unemployment. In neither case will the situation be satisfactory.

A closer look at the processes going on will show that the interaction of the various factors is even more complicated, and there seems to be a tendency for the inflationary forces in the system to become stronger while the forces favorable to employment are becoming weaker. This has to do with two of the features of the market mechanisms that were mentioned above.

In the section "Labor Market Practices" it was stressed that the tendency for wages and prices to continue to rise may appear gradually to have become an autonomous factor in the system. This means that if an upward movement has started, the inflationary forces continue working even after the cessation of the original impulse.

In the section "Concentration and Market Power" the statistics quoted seem to indicate that even in the less concentrated industries the price markups increase during recessions, and in the highly concentrated branches they are particularly high during the recessions. This means that if raw material prices fall in years of weak demand, firms have an opportunity to increase profits so that the prices of the finished products do not fall. They may, in fact, go on rising because of the autonomous tendency for wages in particular, to rise almost regardless of the demand situation.

Under such circumstances what will the effects of an expansion of total demand be? In the first instance inflation will be reinforced, but the employment situation will improve. The autonomous nature of the wage and price rises means that inflation is likely to continue, with a negative effect on employment. In the section "Competing and Sheltered Sectors" it was shown, especially in Table 3.1, that in the competing sector wages tend to rise much more than prices. The first result of this is likely to be a reduction of production. Later, new labor-saving techniques may help industries to survive, though with a somewhat smaller labor force.

This means that the inflationary effect of a demand expansion will tend to continue, to some extent, after the direct impulse resulting from the expansionary measures. The positive influence on employment, on the other hand, will tend to be temporary. The level of unemployment will remain high.

If we now consider the effect of contractionary fiscal and/or monetary measures, we find that the reduction of demand will have a negative influence on the level of employment. The question is what will be the influence on the rate of inflation. The reduction of total demand will weaken the market power of enterprises and labor unions. If, however, price markups are particularly high during recessions, the consequence is likely to be a reduction in sales while prices are maintained or even increased. This will particularly be the case if an autonomous wage increase occurs, so that labor costs are rising.

The conclusion of the above reasoning seems to be that expansionary demand management may be able only temporarily to influence employment in a positive direction, and that the chances of lowering the rates of inflation through restrictive policies are poor. The possibilities of getting out of the present unhappy combination of inflation and unemployment through appropriate demand management must, therefore, be considered small or nonexistent.

The monetarist school of economics, and particularly its founder, Prof. Milton Friedman, has an inclination to talk about a "natural rate of unemployment" that seems unavoidable in the long run. Is this view supported by the analysis undertaken above? One might add another, similar question: Is there not only a natural rate of unemployment but also what could be called a natural rate of inflation, that too being unavoidable?

In my view the word "natural" is misleading in both cases. It is not in the nature of things that there must always be high rates of unemployment or of inflation. Rather, with the present organization of markets and of the public sector, a strong tendency for both inflation and unemployment to be persistent features of modern economies seems to be built into the system. This does not prevent the performance of the system from being better in both respects if these systems of organization are improved. This question will be dealt with in Chapter 6.

In this section it has been necessary to include employment in the reasoning rather extensively because, regarding demand management, the problems of inflation and unemployment are closely related. It was hoped during the first part of the postwar period that wise demand management could bring us close to a society with full employment without inflation. This has not happened so far.

Before we turn to the employment problem in Chapter 4, a few additional aspects of inflation must be considered.

INTERNATIONAL INFLATION PROBLEMS

The growing importance of international transactions has added an international dimension to many problems, and this includes the problem of inflation.

International trade is being influenced by export cartels in many branches. They may consist of the major exporting enterprises in a certain country, but in a number of cases they are international, comprising enterprises from various countries. In both cases the purpose is to strengthen the market power of the participants by limiting competition. Whether this is done by allocation of markets or by agreement on prices, the result will usually be that prices in the importing countries will be higher than they would otherwise have been.

The fact that prices are fixed outside the importing countries makes price control more difficult and complicated. Export cartels therefore represent an extension of the scope of the problems discussed in the section "Concentration and Market Power."

The most powerful export cartel is OPEC, the Organization of Petroleum Exporting Countries. In a few other cases countries exporting primary products have made similar efforts to strengthen their market power by uniting, and this may be of increasing importance in the years to come. Most export cartels have, however, been formed within the manufacturing sector. The general trend toward concentration in industry of course facilitates the formation of such cartels, and they are therefore likely to be of increasing importance.

The price fixing of multinational corporations is another example of the internationalization of market organization. In some respects its effects are similar to those of export cartels, but there are also important differences. The similarity consists in the fact that the important decisions are often made in one country while the goods concerned are sold in other countries.

The main difference is that the last stages of production often take place in the country where the products are sold. Sometimes, however, things are more complicated. The parent company may be situated in one country; part of the end products may be made by subsidiaries in other countries, from which they may be exported to third countries.

The dimensions of these problems are considerable. In 1971 the value added of all multinationals was estimated at approximately one-fifth of the world GNP (excluding centrally planned economies).[9] International production, measured by the sales of foreign subsidiaries of multinational corporations, was larger than the total exports of all market economies. And the importance of multinationals has increased since 1971.

The one element in the working of this large system that is most difficult to control is transfer pricing, the pricing of raw materials and intermediary products traded between parent companies and subsidiaries and between subsidiaries. The effects of the pricing system are felt mainly in the countries where the end products are sold, but the profits earned in these countries may be only modest. There is a natural temptation to fix transfer prices in such a way that profits are concentrated to a large extent in countries where the legislation relating to price control and taxation is favorable. This problem will be discussed further in Chapter 6.

A problem of particular importance is what has been called the international transmission of inflation. This means that changes taking place in some countries have inflationary effects in other countries. The most important of such influences is the transmission of inflation through international trade. If there were only two countries, A and B, and A had inflation while B had not, trade with A would have an inflationary impact on B, because both import and export prices would be rising. Furthermore, inflation in A would make its goods less competitive. Demand would, therefore, increasingly be directed toward the cheaper goods from B, and this increased demand would have an inflationary effect in B. There could also be a capital flow from A to B because firms in A would move some of their production to B, where the costs of production were not rising as they were in A. This capital inflow would increase liquidity in B and thus act as an expansionary change in the monetary policy of that country. And the investments undertaken in B by firms from A would raise the demand for labor and for materials, thus creating an additional inflationary impulse in B.

Countries do not live in isolation. If the trading partners of a certain country have more inflation than that country has, then they are exporting part of their inflation to this country. This is to be taken literally. Returning to the example above, it should be added that what we have looked at so far have been the effects in country B of the trading between the two countries. But what are the effects in country A?

The relations between the two countries will have a dampening effect on the inflation in country A. Trade with country B means that export and import prices in A become lower compared with its internal prices. Producers in country A must, therefore, compete with cheaper foreign products, which reduces their market power.

Just as demand for the cheap products of country B would increase, the corresponding demand for the products of A would decrease. And the capital flow from A to B would reduce liquidity in A, just as it would increase liquidity in B. Finally, corresponding to the increased demand for labor and materials in B, resulting from the investment by firms in A, there must be a reduction of demand in A. What has been said so far means that it would be an oversimplification to say only that country B gets some inflation as there has been inflation in its trading partner A. It must be added that there is some influence in the opposite direction in country A.

Looked at in a broader international perspective, one can draw the conclusion that trade and other transactions have a certain tendency to reduce the differences between the rates of inflation in the countries having such economic relations. This was in fact one of the conclusions of a study undertaken in the OECD in 1973[10]. The first sentences of the summary of this study read as follows:

> A wide-held view is that the increasing international interdependence of the area—and of European economies in particular—has led to a higher degree of 'internationalisation' of the problem of inflation. Some support for this view is in fact found in the reduced dispersion of national inflation that has taken place over the past 15 years, this occurring without a comparable synchronization of demand pressures.

It should be remembered that the study was undertaken in the first part of 1973. Therefore, it only covers the period until about the end of 1972. Since then two factors have been of growing importance, and they have, to a considerable extent, modified the picture of the transmission of inflation.

One of these factors has already been mentioned, namely in the section "Demand Management". The conclusions of that section as regards inflation were: 1. that the inflationary effect of an expansionary demand management was to be of a rather persistent nature because of the existing autonomous nature of wage/price rises. Even a temporary strengthening of the inflationary forces therefore tends to have a more lasting effect. 2. That for similar reasons the weakening of demand through restrictive demand management had rather poor chances of reducing inflation. It would, rather, reduce production and employment.

If we try to apply this kind of reasoning to the two-country example described above, we get the following picture: The difference between the price behavior of countries A and B leads to an expansion of the demand for products and labor in country B, where prices are stable. It also leads to a corresponding reduction of demand in country A, where prices are rising.

An increase in demand is likely to have a lasting inflationary effect. On the other hand, a reduction in demand cannot perceptibly reduce the rate of inflation. It will, rather, reduce production and employment. Transferred to the two-country example, this means that inflation will be increased more in country B than it will be reduced in country A.

Widening the perspective, we may conclude that the growing interdependence of national economies under present market conditions tends to increase the rates of inflation more in countries where they are low than it will reduce these rates where they are high. The net result is, therefore, likely to be that there will be more inflation in the world as a whole. At the same time there will be more unemployment in the countries where the rates of inflation are high. This means that to some extent the transmission process is detrimental to both types of countries. Where prices are stable, some inflation is imported. Where there is high inflation, the reduced competitiveness leads to unemployment.

Both types of countries can defend themselves against these difficulties by changing their exchange rates. Countries with fairly stable prices can protect themselves against imported inflation by revaluing their currencies. This will counteract the increases of import and export prices that result from the inflation of other countries. Countries having high inflation can improve their reduced competitiveness by devaluing their currencies. This will lower the prices of their products, measured in other currencies, and thus help them to acquire larger market shares at home and abroad. As a consequence their production and employment will increase, as long as they do not spoil their situation again by having too much inflation.

The fact that exchange rates are changed frequently is the second new feature in the evolution of the international community since 1973. Market mechanisms have been strengthened, and thus have become more inflationary in their effects. At the same time, the international monetary system has changed. Changes in exchange rates have played an increasing role, often through more or less controlled floating.

After the dollar crisis in August 1971, the major Western countries tried, through the Smithsonian Agreement in December of that year, to establish a new system of exchange rates that in principle were fixed. This effort failed in 1973, and since then both floating and deliberate changes of exchange rates have frequently taken place.

It is important to note that the breakdown of the system of fixed exchange rates took place several months before the first oil price rise in 1973-74. This shows that countries were not able to manage this system. There was too much inflation or too much unemployment in many countries, and the transmission of inflation did not solve these problems. The oil price rise has of course, further complicated the situation. It represents a new inflationary impulse, and it has seriously deteriorated the balance of payments of many oil-importing countries.

It is important to emphasize that the floating of exchange rates may have a dangerous inflationary impact in countries where the currency is moving downward.

A deliberate devaluation can improve the competitiveness of a country, provided it is accompanied by measures to stop or reduce the inflation that made the devaluation necessary. This is no easy task, because the devaluation itself has a direct inflationary impact on the economy. It means that import and export prices become higher, measured in the national currency. This will raise the national price level; and if wages are raised, a new wage/price spiral may start, which may further weaken the competitiveness of the country.

These effects can be counteracted if the devaluation is supported by an effective incomes policy that keeps the cost level as close to stability as possible. Perhaps a restrictive fiscal policy will also be needed to keep the level of total demand sufficiently low.

If, on the contrary, exchange rates are floating, they will change from day to day, particularly if the floating is uncontrolled. In that case there is no possibility of taking supporting measures each time the international value of a currency moves up or down. The inflationary effects of a downward movement of the currency therefore cannot be counteracted effectively.

It has been said, in defense of floating rates, that they permit the value of a currency to move toward its "natural" level. But what actually happens when the exchange rate of a currency moves down is that the "natural" value is pushed downward too. If the exchange rate of a currency falls because there is too much inflation in the country concerned, its fall will reinforce this inflation. The "natural" value is therefore not a well-defined, fixed magnitude. If the exchange rate of a currency is floating, its "natural" value will be floating too.

Floating exchange rates have, therefore, on the whole been a destabilizing factor in the international monetary system. This will remain true as long as market mechanisms are uncontrollable because wages and prices have an autonomous upward drift.

The result of the interaction of the various factors discussed above has been that since 1973 there has been no reduction in the dispersion of national rates of inflation. On the contrary, not only have the average rates of inflation in OECD member countries been high, even in years when the real price of oil has declined slightly; the gaps between the national inflation rates have also, on the whole, been widening.

Table 3.3 outlines the development of inflation rates in the OECD member countries from 1961 to 1979. For each period the lowest and the highest rates in the 24 countries are shown, as are the rates for the seven major countries, whose impact on the others is particularly important.

This table clearly shows that the gap between the lowest and the highest rates of inflation has become much wider since the first part of the period. Also, the gaps between the major countries have widened. For two reasons this is a fact of general importance. One of the reasons is that in the interaction of trade and capital movements, the influences emanating from the larger countries are particularly strong. The other is that many countries, including several countries of the South, have linked their currencies in some way to the currency of a major country. Many national societies therefore are exposed to disturbances if the currency to which their own is linked becomes unstable.

THE NEW CAUSES OF INFLATION: SUMMARY

It may be useful to summarize the main arguments of the analysis undertaken above. The main purpose has been to explain why inflation has become a persistent feature of modern economies during the postwar period, and increasingly so from the mid-1960s.

The active element in this new type of development has been the growing organization of the product and labor markets. Many enterprises have gotten a degree of market power that was rare in former times. Enterprises became large in several branches and their techniques became sophisticated and capital-intensive. This represented both a force and a risk. It was a force because often a few of these large enterprises dominated the market, and each gave its products a special image. They therefore could raise their prices without reducing sales substantially, especially when labor costs had increased.

But there was also a risk because of the large fixed costs that had to be covered even during a strike or lockout. Therefore, though such enterprises could be strong in the product markets, they were

TABLE 3.3: Percentage Rates of Inflation in OECD Countries, 1961-70 to 1979

	1961-70	*1971-76*	*1977*	*1978*	*1979*	*6 months to Dec. 1979*
Lowest rate	2.2	6.6	1.3	1.1	3.6	2.1
Highest rate	11.9	26.0	29.9	61.9	63.5	94.5
United States	2.8	6.6	6.5	7.7	11.3	12.7
Japan	5.8	11.1	8.1	3.8	3.6	5.3
Germany	2.7	5.9	3.7	2.7	4.1	4.2
France	4.0	8.9	9.4	9.1	10.8	12.3
United Kingdom	4.1	13.6	15.9	8.3	13.4	18.8
Canada	2.7	7.4	8.0	9.0	9.1	9.0
Italy	3.9	12.2	17.0	12.1	14.8	21.2
Total OECD	3.4	8.6	8.7	7.9	9.9	11.9

Source: "Latest Trends in Consumer Prices," press release (Paris: OECD, Feb. 1980).

relatively weak in the labor market. Instead of risking the loss of market shares during a strike, they often found it preferable to accept wage rises that they could pass on to the consumers through price rises. This is why labor unions have been so strong in recent decades, but their growing strength is also due to an increasing degree of organization of the labor force.

In this way the postwar period has been characterized by growing market power of a large part of industry and of labor unions, and both have contributed to an increasing tendency to push prices and wages upward all the time.

The large firms usually belong to the so-called competing sector, taking part in foreign trade. In a large part of this sector competition is limited because of the increasing concentration in many industries. This trend has been strengthened by the growing importance of multinational corporations whose transactions are not easily controlled.

In the sheltered sector, most enterprises are small. However, competition in retail trade and services has probably never been perfect, and the fact that many of these small firms are now united in associations has made it easier for them than in earlier periods to pass a large part of the wage rises on to consumers.

As already mentioned, governments in many countries have regulated the agricultural markets so that prices can follow the upward trend in other parts of the economy. They also have supported labor unions by allowing a growing part of unemployment compensation to be financed by the public sector.

The picture is, therefore, almost complete. Large parts of the product and labor markets are now organized to such an extent that there is a persistent tendency for wages and prices to be pushed upward even when there is a great deal of unemployment. At least regarding wages one probably can, in many countries, begin to talk of an autonomous upward movement, something that is taken for granted even in years when the economic situation is bad.

This, then, has been the new active element in the economic systems. Other parts of these systems have passively adapted themselves to the inflationary tendencies thus created.

One of the consequences of rising costs and prices is that the transactions taking place in society represent increasing sums of money. The new organization of capital markets described in Chapter 2 has, therefore, indirectly supported this price/cost-push inflation by making it relatively easy to borrow. The amount of international liquidity has been growing fast, and in the individual countries, governments and central banks would be criticized if monetary policy were so restrictive that transactions at higher prices and wages could be financed only if the quantities were reduced. Such a reduction would mean more unemployment, and the authorities therefore have been under pressure. The quantity of money in circulation had to be increased sufficiently to permit transactions to be carried out at higher prices and wages, and representing the same quantities as before.

This means that the active factor behind the inflation has been the market power obtained in the product and labor markets. The capital markets have more passively adapted themselves to the changed situation. The same can be said about the public sector. As indicated above, when market power in the product and labor markets has created inflation, the central bank will usually have to follow suit by permitting the amount of money in circulation to increase correspondingly.

At the same time the political authorities have to accept that fiscal policy cannot be used to reduce the rate of inflation in any perceptible way. There is even a danger that it can reinforce inflation without reducing unemployment appreciably when expansionary policies are pursued. This was explained in the section "Demand Management," where it was also indicated that in recent years the situation seems to have become more serious because continued wage increases are becoming an autonomous process. And in large parts of the economy wage increases are followed by price increases.

Thus, an element of asymmetry has come into the system, as illustrated in Figure 3.1.

Figure 3.1. A illustrates the system as it was thought to work in the 1950s. There would never be complete price stability or full employment, but there was symmetry in the system. Through an expansionary policy one could move from a toward b. There would then be more inflation but less unemployment. If a contractionary policy was then pursued, one would move backward toward a, and there would again be more unemployment but less inflation. Figure 3.1.B illustrates the system as it increasingly seems to be working because the wage/price spiral is becoming a more autonomous process.

This being so, an expansionary policy will create more inflation but unemployment will not be reduced very much. If then, from point b, a contractionary policy is started, unemployment will again increase but the rate of inflation will be reduced only slightly because the autonomous wage/price rise will continue. A new expansionary policy will now start a movement from c toward d, and so on.

FIGURE 3.1: Inflation and Unemployment

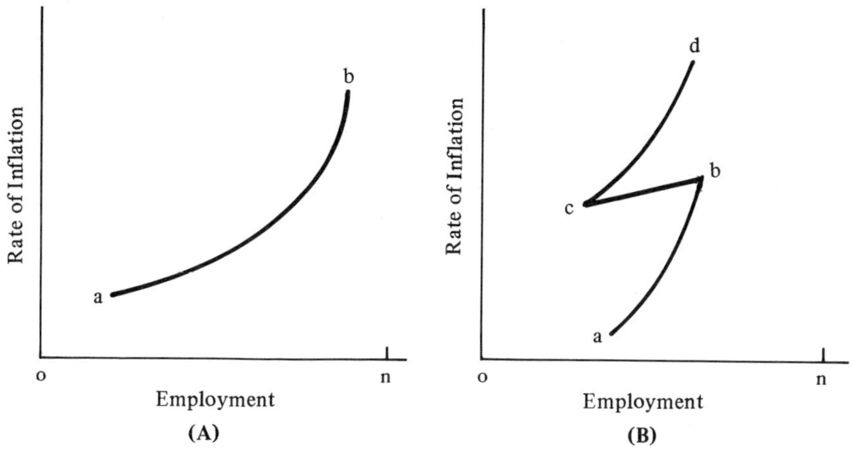

Note: o = price stability
n = full employment
Source: Constructed by the author.

Thus, the working of the system has become asymmetric. The effect of a contractionary policy is not simply the opposite of that of an expansion, since the element of inflation in the process is not reversible. This is a consequence of the fact that enterprises and labor unions that have any market power are inclined to react to an expansion of demand by raising prices and wages, while they will usually respond to a reduction of demand by accepting reduced sales and employment rather than reduced prices and wages. In fact, wages and prices may continue to rise, though more slowly than in years of expanding demand.

This attitude is indirectly supported by the public sector, which now finances most of the unemployment compensation in most modern societies. As indicated earlier, the public sector has also helped agriculture make its prices follow the general trend through regulation of the market.

But, it may be asked, is it not so that the public sector—or, rather, the political system—has counteracted inflation by introducing price control? This is what has happened increasingly in recent decades. There are, however, some important weaknesses in the systems of price control as they function today.

One is the fact that national price control systems have only limited possibilities regarding prices in international trade. They are particularly weak as regards transfer pricing in multinational corporations. If such a corporation has factories in, say, 80 countries and exports to 40 other countries, none of the governments can control what the entire corporation, including all its subsidiaries, has earned.

The other weakness of the systems of price control is that they do not comprise wages, though the price of labor is the most important of all prices. In a typical modern society wages represent between 60 and 70 percent of GNP.

The problems regarding price and wage policies will be treated in Chapter 6.

The international monetary system has also, on the whole, adapted itself passively to the inflationary tendencies created by the market power of products and labor. The system established at the end of World War II and whose center was the International Monetary Fund (IMF) was intended to contain a considerable element of discipline. Changes in a rate of exchange beyond certain limits required the approval of the IMF; and though countries having balance-of-payments deficits could draw foreign currencies from the IMF, such drawings were subject to conditions of increasing severity as the amounts drawn became greater.

This system worked reasonably well during the first part of the postwar period; but when inflation gathered momentum during the 1960s and 1970s, it became exposed to growing pressures. In the early months of 1973 it broke down. Since then the IMF has not been able to control the floating of exchange rates; and though it can still stipulate conditions for drawings beyond certain limits, it has seldom had an occasion to do so because the ample liquidity of the international capital market has made it possible for countries to finance a balance-of-payments deficit for a long period without asking the IMF for support.

It has already been shown that uncontrolled floating of exchange rates favors inflation. And the fact that many countries have been able to run a balance-of-payments deficit for years has meant that inflationary tendencies are not counteracted at an early stage, as was intended in 1945.

We can, therefore, conclude that the growing market power of large parts of the business sector and of labor unions is the main, active factor behind the new tendency for inflation to become a persistent feature of modern economies. And that the other important factors of the systems have been permissive in this respect.

It is thought-provoking that the capital markets, the public sector in national economies, and the international monetary system have passively adapted themselves to the new inflationary climate created by growing market power. By doing this, they have indirectly supported the forces leading to inflation.

CONSEQUENCES OF INFLATION

One of the reasons why policy makers have accepted inflation to an exceedingly high degree may be that too little has been done to make it clear what the consequences for society will be if this tendency is allowed to continue, and perhaps become even stronger, in the years to come.

Modern economies are to a large extent monetary economies. Nearly all transactions consist of something being exchanged for money. Therefore, in each individual country the national currency is the unit in which the economic value of all the objects that can be exchanged is measured.

This being so, it must have far-reaching consequences when the real value of the unit of value is falling to a considerable extent. This is, in fact, what inflation means. When the price level is rising, one monetary unit is worth smaller and smaller quantities of goods and services and of real capital assets, such as land, houses, ships, and machinery.

One direct consequence is that the real value of a debt, denominated in money, is falling. Interest and repayment represent declining quantities of goods of every kind. Therefore, debtors gain by inflation and creditors lose. This is one of the most important direct consequences of an inflationary development.

Who are the debtors in a modern society, and who are the creditors? Only to a very modest extent are the debtors poor people in a difficult position. As a general rule they are persons and corporations who own houses, factories, and other real capital partly financed by borrowing from banks and other institutions granting credit. The creditors do not belong to any special group. Both enterprises and individuals need liquid funds. Most of these funds will be deposited in banks or savings banks but some have invested part of their savings in bonds.

It would be of great interest to know how the gains and losses caused by inflation are distributed among the various groups of the population. A study of this problem has been undertaken for Denmark, a fairly typical modern society.[11] In this study the relation between the money assets owned by the various groups and the debts owed by them has been calculated on the basis of statistical material available. This money assets/debt ratio in 1973 was as follows for the most important groups of the population: entrepreneurs, 0.70; employees, 0.85; workers, 1.24; pensioners, 4.11.

The first two groups had net gains from the process of inflation because their debts exceeded the value of their money assets. This could be expected for entrepreneurs because farmers, merchants, and owners of small factories have invested most of their funds in real capital of various kinds. That it was also true of employees is explained by the fact that in Denmark many employees own the houses in which they live, and these houses are usually mortgaged to a considerable extent. Workers and pensioners are net losers, since many of them do not own houses or other kinds of real capital. What wealth they have, therefore, consists mainly of money assets, such as deposits in banks or savings banks, and in some cases of bonds.

This study seems, therefore, to confirm the general impression that those who gain by inflation are mainly people who are already relatively well off, while those who lose generally belong to groups with lower incomes. In this way inflation contributes to widening the gaps between the various income groups in society. It is one of the reasons why there is more inequality in the distribution of wealth than in the distribution of incomes.

The study just referred to deals only with persons. A large part of the real capital is owned by corporations that have financed many of their activities by borrowing. Therefore, they usually have much more debt than money assets. As a consequence they gain by inflation, probably more so than entrepreneurs do.

It was stressed earlier that the profits of enterprises have declined in recent years. It can now be added that part of this loss has been counterbalanced by inflation gains that have been substantial in many cases.

One further consequence of persistent inflation is that it creates the expectation of continued inflation in the future, and this is bound to influence people's actions. In particular it encourages both individuals and corporations to invest as much as possible in real capital, because then they escape the loss by continued inflation that they would suffer if the same amounts were invested in money assets. If they borrow part of the money they want to invest in various types of real capital assets, they can at the same time obtain an inflation gain as debtors. And the possession of the real capital assets that they have bought permits them to give security for more loans to banks or other lenders.

As a consequence, the prices of assets that are particularly attractive in a period of inflation tend to be pulled upward by demand that is provoked by the inflation itself. Their prices will, therefore, often rise more than the price level in general.

Some examples of this tendency are given in the Danish study cited above. In Denmark, if prices in 1960 were set at 100, they had increased to the following levels in 1973: vacant lots, 1,107; houses, 439; farms, 341; consumer prices, 218. Obviously the prices of these types of assets have increased a great deal more than has the general price index.

This has unfortunate consequences. If a young family is to buy a house or a farm, it has to pay a price that is high in relation to prices in general and, therefore, often high in relation to the incomes they can expect to earn during the next few years.

At the same time, if they have to borrow much of the money needed to buy the house or the farm, they will for reasons explained below have to pay interest rates that are very high because of the same inflation that has made the house or the farm so expensive. They will, therefore, have a hard time during the first years after the purchase. The same may be true of young people who want to start an enterprise in an area other than agriculture.

People with initiative and new ideas may for these reasons be prevented from making innovations that would be valuable for society but would require more capital than they own or can borrow. On the other hand, a person who has owned a house or a farm during 20 or 30 years of inflation may be able to sell it at a real price substantially higher than the price at which it was bought. And in the meantime that person will have had an inflation gain in his or her capacity as a debtor.

Inflation therefore represents a discrimination against those who are going to start a new enterprise and in favor of those who have been in business for many years. Consequently, people tend to stay in business too long because, when they retire and become pensioners, they will begin to lose from further inflation as mentioned above.

In these ways inflation can be harmful to initiative and innovation. It probably has not been sufficiently recognized what the consequences of this are likely to be in the long run.

Just as it can be advantageous to buy real capital assets in a period of inflation, it can be tempting to get rid of money assets whose real value will go down if inflation continues. There will, therefore, be a temptation to sell securities and withdraw money from banks and savings banks in order to purchase houses and other real capital assets. As indicated above, there will also be a temptation to borrow more money for the same purposes.

This means that the rates of interest will become higher because of continued inflation. The prices of bonds will fall when there is a general tendency to sell them, and so their effective rates will rise. In order to compete with these higher effective rates, banks and savings banks must raise their interest rates on deposits, and therefore interest on loans will also become higher. The tendency to withdraw money from banks and to borrow more from them works in the same direction.

It is, however, a notable fact that rates of interest do not rise so much during periods of inflation that those who have money assets get full compensation for the annual loss of the purchasing power of money. This is because there are limits to the possibility of getting rid of money assets in order to buy real capital assets, the prices of which are supposed to rise. It is necessary for all people to have some money of which they can dispose at short notice, and for enterprises it can be important to have large amounts available at any time.

To this must be added the fact that explains why many workers and pensioners have more money assets than debts. Only those who are relatively wealthy can afford to buy a house. For those who cannot do this, the only possibility of keeping their savings in a convenient form is to deposit them in a bank or savings bank.

For these reasons even a long period of inflation will make interest rates rise only to such an extent that the real rates of interest are extremely low when the declining purchasing power of money is taken into account.

Table 3.4 shows the long-term rate of interest in December 1979

TABLE 3.4: Rates of Interest and Inflation; Eight Countries, June-December 1979

Country	*Rate of Inflation*	*Rate of Interest*
Switzerland	2.1	4.04
Germany	4.2	8.08
Japan	5.3	8.61
Netherlands	5.7	8.14
France	12.3	12.59
United States	12.7	11.35
United Kingdom	18.8	14.72
Italy	21.2	14.27

Sources: OECD, *Financial Market Trends* no. 13 (Feb. 1980): 88; "Latest Trends in Consumer Prices," press release (Paris: OECD, Feb. 1980).

in eight countries, compared with the annual rate of inflation (consumer prices) of the same countries during June to December 1979.

It will be seen that as a general rule the countries that have high rates of inflation also have high rates of interest. But when the rates of inflation rise, the rates of interest do not rise correspondingly. Therefore, in the countries with the highest rates of inflation, the real rates of interest are negative, very much so in Italy.

In fact, what matters for those who borrow, as well as for those who buy bonds or deposit money in banks, is the real rates of interest after taxes. These are, of course, even lower than those that appear in the table. How much lower they are depends on the tax legislation of the country in question and on the economic situation of the person concerned. There can be no doubt, however, that in most of the countries shown in the table, the real rate of interest after taxes will be negative for many depositors and for many borrowers as well.

This has two important consequences. One is that the gains obtained by borrowers and the losses suffered by depositors during a period of inflation are even higher than indicated in the first part of this section. The high rates of taxation in most modern societies tend to reinforce the discrimination against people with modest means at their disposal, a situation that is created by inflation.

The other consequence is that borrowing to invest in real capital has become extremely cheap because of inflation. The first years after the borrowing may be hard for, say, a young farmer, but a corporation with strong market power will find the real costs of new investment extremely low. In addition, the rules regarding depreciation allowance in tax legislation are often formulated in such a way that taxes are reduced considerably during the first years after substantial investment has been made.

There can be no doubt that these facts, combined with the rising costs of labor, have acted as a strong inducement to replace labor by capital through investment in labor-saving machinery and other equipment. In this way inflation has been one of the causes of the unemployment that began to increase during the second half of the 1960s. In a country like Denmark, real rates of interest after taxes have been negative since 1961 for many people.

What has been dealt with so far is consequences of inflation in a single country. There are also important international consequences of inflation. In the section "International Inflation Problems" it was argued that the transmission of inflation works in such a way that rates of inflation are increased more in countries where they are low than they are lowered in countries where they are high.

If this is true, the fact that rates of inflation differ between countries should tend to raise the average level of inflation. This tendency is aggravated by the fact that in a period when general forces tend to create inflation, some national economies are able to resist these forces much more effectively than others. Switzerland and West Germany are cases in point.

It is, therefore, not surprising that the recent period of generally rising rates of inflation has also been a period of increasing differences between national rates of inflation. This in turn has contributed to the gradual breakdown of the international monetary system, based on fixed but adjustable rates of exchange. As a result, we have a system dominated by exchange rates that are floating to a high degree, and this includes the fact that the relations between the few currencies that are of decisive importance to the world economy have been changing in a rather uncontrolled way since the breakdown in 1973.

It was explained earlier that floating rates have an inherent tendency to further inflation. This is particularly true in countries where the floating is uncontrolled and where the resistance against inflationary forces is weak.

This brings us to the last point to be dealt with in this chapter. If the argumentation of this chapter is reasonably correct, the postwar inflation that has gathered momentum from the second half of the 1960s is more dangerous than has been recognized in much of the public discussion.

This may have to do with the fact that the period has been troublesome in various other respects too. A fact that may tend to divert the attention of most people from the problems of inflation. And in an individual country, inflation becomes more acceptable when other countries have inflation too.

It is, therefore, important to stress that some of the factors discussed in this chapter reinforce one another. Inflation in many countries gives rise to floating rates of exchange, and floating rates tend to facilitate further inflation. Under such circumstances, expectations of continued inflation tend to become strong, and they tend to strengthen the inflationary forces—for instance, by making the wage/price spiral an autonomous factor.

There is, therefore, undeniably a danger that the inflation of modern societies may become accelerating in many countries. If it should become accelerating in some of the major countries, this could disturb other parts of the international community.

In Chapter 4 it will be argued that the forces that have created this new, persistent inflation are also some of the strongest forces behind the new, persistent unemployment that has developed during the same period. It will, therefore, be necessary to come back to these forces in the last chapter of this book.

NOTES

1. OECD, *Inflation, the Present Problem* (Paris: OECD, 1970), p. 24.
2. Gösta Edgren, Karl-Olof Faxén, and Clas-Erik Odhner, *Wage Formation and the Economy*, (London: Allen and Unwin, 1973).
3. OECD, *Concentration and Competition Policy* (Paris: OECD, 1979), p. 138.
4. Dennis Swann, *Competition and Consumer Protection (Harmondsworth: Penguin Books, 1979), p. 138.*
5. Howard M. Wachtel and Peter D. Adelsheim, "How Recession Feeds Inflation: Price Markups in a Concentrated Economy," *Challenge* (Sept.-Oct. 1977): 6-13.
6. Swann, loc. cit.
7. Paolo Sylos-Labrini, "Prices and Income Distribution in Manufacturing Industry," *Journal of Post-Keynesian Economics* 2, no. 1 (1979): 3-25.
8. OECD, *Economic Outlook* no. 15 (1974), Table 13.
9. OECD, *Restrictive Business Practices of Multinational Enterprises* (Paris: OECD, 1977), p. 10.
10. OECD Economic Outlook No. 13, *The International Transmission of Inflation* (Paris: OECD, July 1973), pp. 81-96.
11. Lars Eskesen, "Formueforskydninger og Inflation," *Nationaløkonomisk Tidsskrift* 113 (1975): 279-93 (summary in English, p. 279).

4

UNEMPLOYMENT

HISTORICAL BACKGROUND

The unemployment problem as we know it today is, on the whole, related to the development of the modern industrial society.

In the oldest agricultural villages there was no labor market. All the inhabitants lived on the farms and took part in the work to be done there. The quantity of work varied according to the season, but that did not mean that some people might lose their living, even temporarily. All the members of a family shared the produce of their farm.

With the emergence of handicrafts, the distinction between the employer and the employed became more explicit. Nevertheless, for a long period the journeymen were fairly closely related to the families of the master artisans, and there was no very clear class distinction.

The start of manufacturing industry led to two important changes in society. For the first time in history, a real working class began to develop, and the social distance between the workers and the captains of industry was radically different from the one that had existed between the master artisan and his journeymen. No wonder that the first socialist ways of thinking developed in the early days of industry.

The other new feature that characterized the industrial society was the growing importance of investment in buildings and machinery. It is in the nature of investment that it fluctuates more than consumption does. Therefore, the business cycles, with alternating short periods of prosperity and depression, are a product of the industrial society.

With the business cycles came unemployment, as mentioned in Chapter 1. As shown in Table 1.2, unemployment moved up and down in a fairly regular way, and the fluctuations were more pronounced in the branches of industry that were related to investment than in those that produced consumer goods.

Gradually, industry became more concentrated, enterprises became larger and larger, and the methods of production more capital-intensive. At the same time the labor markets were gradually being organized and the public sector became a factor of growing importance. The modern society was beginning to emerge.

During the Great Depression of the 1930s, unemployment reached unusually high levels and lasted longer than during earlier depressions. Economists who have tried to analyze the Great Depression have given many causes for it. I shall not try to offer any new theory, but it may be appropriate to mention that the types of organization that have become so important following World War II were already on their way during the interwar period. If more expansionary policies had been pursued, as suggested by John Maynard Keynes, there might have been a somewhat lower rate of unemployment, but there would probably have been more inflation.

Society is changing all the time. Several national economies were only imperfectly stabilized after World War I, and some of the rigidities that have characterized the postwar period already existed during the 1930s. The nature of the Great Depression may have something to do with both these facts.

During the postwar period the labor market has become more organized, and the nature of the labor force itself has changed in various ways. First of all, the number of entrepreneurs, those who personally own an enterprise, has been reduced, and more and more people have become wage earners.* The large enterprises are now owned by corporations, and many people are employed by the public sector.

At the same time, the labor force has become more differentiated. There are skilled workers of various kinds, and most of the so-called unskilled workers do in fact have some skills, often of a specific nature. The most important change that has taken place during the last few decades is, however, the development of a growing staff of employees of various ranks, including the presidents of large corporations.

Table 4.1 shows the composition of the labor force of a small, modern society in 1976. The situation revealed in this table is

*Where nothing else is indicated, this term will include salary earners.

noteworthy in several respects. The entrepreneurs were only 13.2 percent of the total labor force. In 1940 they accounted for 25.5 percent and numbered 418,700. This decline reflects a growing concentration, with enterprises becoming larger both in agriculture and in industry and trade.

The incomes of entrepreneurs shown in the table may seem surprisingly low compared with those of important groups of employees. It is interesting to note in this respect that 64 percent of the entrepreneurs employed no wage earners at all. They were small farmers, shopkeepers, taxi owners, hairdressers, and so on, many of whom had fairly low incomes. If one thinks in terms of "the conflict between capital and labor," it should be remembered that the true representatives of capital are today a minority of entrepreneurs—and, of course, the corporations whose presidents are a kind of wage earners.

There are now more employees than workers in the Danish labor force, and the number of them has grown dramatically. In 1940 there were more than twice as many workers as employees. Part of the explanation can be found in the expansion of the public sector, which now employs about 30 percent of the total labor force. Many of the people engaged in the public sector have the status of employees. In

TABLE 4.1: Labor Force of Denmark, 1976

	Number (thousand)	*Income (1,000 kroner)*[a]
Entrepreneurs	338.1	91.6
Presidents	8.7	262.2
Superior officials	126.3	143.5
Higher employees	290.2	91.3
Other employees	433.7	64.8
Total employees	858.9	87.3
Skilled workers	301.2	73.4
Unskilled workers	483.9	62.4
Total workers	785.1	66.6
Unspecified wage earners[b]	353.3	48.1
Total labor force	2,535.4	74.4

[a] 1 krone = U.S. $0.18.

[b] Undoubtedly including part-time workers.

Source: Statistiske Efterretninger no. A 1978-22 (1978).

private industry too, the employees have become an important part of the enterprises, as is shown by the growing role that salaries play (see Table 3.2).

In Table 4.1 employees are divided into four groups. Those of the higher grades usually constitute a particularly important part of the establishment, to which they will often be fairly closely linked.

In a more general way the salaries of employees to a large extent represent fixed costs to the enterprises. The growing role of fixed labor costs has been mentioned in Chapter 3. The variable labor costs of workers (and sometimes of part of the lower grades of employees), therefore, often give an imperfect picture of the situation. This should be remembered when the relations between wages and prices are discussed.

It may be appropriate to conclude this short description of the labor force with some remarks about the particular vulnerability of those who earn their living by offering their labor for sale. Of the three categories of markets discussed in this book, the labor markets are unique in one respect. If demand is declining in the product markets, enterprises can protect themselves by reducing production, thereby adjusting supply to demand. In the capital markets there is no unemployment problem. All the existing liquidity or financial capital is "employed" somewhere at any given time. Those who have money at their disposal can invest it in real capital or in stocks, or deposit it in banks. If the market situation of their investments deteriorates, investors can move their funds to other assets.

In the labor markets the situation is different. The great majority of those who offer their labor for sale have no other possibility of earning a living. And in the present highly organized labor markets they cannot be sure that they will get a job by lowering their price. The price has been fixed by the organizations.

It is, therefore, a real problem for modern societies that often many people are unemployed because the market cannot absorb the existing supply of labor. Unemployment compensation can be used to alleviate the living conditions of those hit by the lack of demand. But unemployment represents a waste of resources, and it demonstrates an imperfection in the working of the economic system. The employment problem has, therefore, become a subject of growing concern in recent years.

THEORIES OF EMPLOYMENT

Roughly speaking, economic thinking developed into a systematic scientific activity during the same phase of history that saw the emergence of the manufacturing industry and of a working class. Society gradually became more complicated.

The United Kingdom was the first country to become industrialized, and it was probably not mere chance that the first dominant school of economic thought also had its origins in that country. The classical school of economics is considered to have been founded by Adam Smith, who, with his best-known follower, David Ricardo, was a British economist.

The classical, and with some modifications the more recent neoclassical, school was based on a reasoning that assumed almost full employment was the normal state of the economy. If employment was reduced, self-adjusting forces would tend to bring the economy back to a state of equilibrium at full employment.

As can be seen from Table 1.2, this kind of theory was a fairly reasonable description of the ways in which the systems worked during the last decades of the 19th century and the first part of the 20th century. However, during the Great Depression of the 1930s, the economies did not work that way. It therefore became necessary to try to explain why an economy could remain for years in a position of high unemployment.

It was this explanation that Keynes tried to give in his *General Theory of Employment, Interest and Money*. He attacked the reasoning of the classical school, his main argument being that the economy could be in equilibrium at less than full employment. There was no reason to believe that self-adjusting forces would bring about full employment, and of course the persistent unemployment during the Great Depression supported this reasoning.

The second lasting contribution made by Keynes in his book was his political argument that since the economy could not be expected automatically to move back to full employment, the authorities had to intervene. He made a great effort to show that the idea of laissez-faire as an appropriate policy in modern economies was groundless.

The instrument that Keynes advocated was demand management. Through monetary and fiscal policies the authorities were to see to it that the level of total demand was high enough to ensure full employment. The weak point in the theory was that Keynes did not convincingly demonstrate that lack of demand was almost the only reason why employment in the 1930s remained at a low level. Still less did he prove that in a situation of persistent unemployment, lack of demand will always be the main cause of that evil. Therefore, the title of the book, *The General Theory of Employment, . . .* is misleading. It is not a general theory that is valid at all times and in all societies. It is a more specific theory, strongly influenced by the situation of the United Kingdom during the 1930s.

The theory lacks a thorough analysis of how market mechanisms in a modern society work. Keynes often expressed his views on the capital market and the rate of interest, but his ideas about the markets for goods and labor were not clear. The following statement from the *General Theory* is probably the most precise one he made about these two markets:

> It follows, therefore, that if labour were to respond to conditions of gradually diminishing employment by offering its services at a gradually diminishing money-wage, this would not, as a rule, have the effect of reducing real wages.[1]

This seems to indicate that, on the whole, Keynes expected prices and wages to move up and down in the same proportion.

That this was really his view has been confirmed by John Hicks, who knew Keynes well. In his book *The Crisis in Keynesian Economics* he writes:

> . . . a principle, very important to Keynes, which I shall call the *wage-theorem*. When there is a general (proportional) rise in money wages, says the theorem, the *normal* is that all prices rise in the same proportion.[2]

Keynes's view on this important point was not based on any detailed argumentation about the functioning of the markets for goods and labor. This may have to do with the fact that the part of economics in which Keynes was particularly interested was monetary theory. R. F. Harrod states in his biography of Keynes that the subject of money was "preeminently his own field," and he describes *A Treatise on Money* as Keynes's most mature work.[3]

It has been a great influence on postwar thinking that Keynes, an economist of genius, could maintain that changes in the price of labor were not an important factor in determining the quantity of labor that could be sold, because other prices would move in the same proportion. It so happened that, all things considered, unemployment was not a serious problem during the first part of the postwar period. Reconstruction after the war was favorable to employment. So were the expansionary policies that were pursued, partly influenced by Keynes, and that became dominant after 1960. Inflation was, however, a problem of growing importance, and therefore more new thinking developed about this than about the problem of unemployment.

A new school of thought, monetarism, was not fundamentally different from Keynes's thinking in regard to employment. It put the main emphasis on the quantity of money, which should be managed in such a way that it would grow in harmony with the long-term trend of the production capacity of society. This is also a kind of demand management.

As mentioned in Chapter 3, according to this school of thought there was a natural level of unemployment that had to be accepted. It was, however, also demonstrated there, in the section "Demand Management," that alternating expansionary and contractionary fiscal and monetary policies run the risk of aggravating the problems of inflation and of unemployment if nothing else is done to improve the working of the system.

Monetarists showed little interest in short-term fluctuations. These have been dealt with more thoroughly by a more recent school of thought, Post-Keynesianism. This represents a refined thinking in various ways. In the essential field of employment and its relations to wages, it seems, however, to follow the ideas of Keynes rather closely. A post-Keynesian economist, Alfred S. Eichner, has expressed this in the following way:

> Post Keynesian short-period models assume that employment depends primarily on aggregate economic output, with any change in the wage rate, either in nominal or in real terms, exerting little or no separate influence.[4]

Here, as with Keynes himself, total demand is decisive and the price of labor of little or no importance. However, as indicated above, demand management is not enough to ensure a satisfactory level of employment. We therefore need a revised theory of employment. It should be based on an analysis of the working of the market mechanisms as they function in the present phase of the evolution of modern societies. It is such a theory that I have tried to outline in the remaining parts of this book.

A REVISED THEORY OF EMPLOYMENT

As indicated above, Keynes's theory was influenced by the situation existing during the Great Depression of the 1930s. His book was therefore, in spite of its title, not a truly general theory of employment, valid at all times and for all types of societies. A general theory in this sense probably will never be formulated. At any time the level of employment will be a result of the working of the existing market mechanisms, influenced by the public sector and by international relations. A theory of employment should, therefore, reflect these conditions of employment creation as they are when the theory is formulated.

What follows is, therefore, only an effort to outline a theory that corresponds to these conditions as they exist in modern societies in the years around 1980. The situation has been very unsatisfactory for a number of years. There is, therefore, a serious need for changes in the working of the systems concerned. These policy issues will be discussed more fully in Chapter 6, but it should be said in advance that the policy problems are part of the theory. A complete theory should consider both how the system works and how its working might be changed if certain policy decisions were made.

Even if Keynes's theory had been fully correct in 1936, when it was formulated, it would not be satisfactory around 1980, because the economic systems have changed. More market power is held by large enterprises and labor unions. Fixed costs are playing an increasing role and in many cases direct labor costs play a more modest role. The role of the public sector has been enlarged, but demand management through fiscal and monetary policies has become more difficult, for the reasons discussed in Chapter 3. To this must be added that because of the oil price rises, balance-of-payments deficits have become a burden in many countries. Demand management will, therefore, often have to be more restrictive than might be desirable from the point of view of employment.

A revised theory must take these historical changes into account. Further changes may occur in the years to come, and it will be argued in Chapter 6 that some important modifications in the working of the systems will be needed if the employment situation is to be improved substantially. Politically, these modifications will be difficult to carry out, and I am afraid that the picture shown below will be fairly close to the truth for quite a number of years. Nevertheless, any theory of employment should be compared with the facts now and earlier.

The first task will be to see how the working of the present system influences the level and pattern of employment. From that point of view we shall look at the product and labor markets, the capital markets, the public sector, and international relations. After that we shall consider how the system reacts to certain changes in the conditions under which it has to work. Changes in three important factors will be considered: technology, the international division of labor, and the rates of economic growth.

These three categories of changes can at large be characterized as exogenous factors, which influence the system from outside, while changes in wages, prices, and other elements of the system itself are endogenous factors. The dividing line between endogenous and exogenous factors is not sharp. Nevertheless, it is, roughly speaking, correct to consider the first part of the outline below as a study of the working of the system itself and the second part as a study of its reactions to outside influences.

THE WORKING OF THE SYSTEMS

Product and Labor Markets

An analysis of the working of the product and labor markets is a particularly important part of this study. It is fairly easy to understand that the market power of enterprises and labor unions tends to push prices and wages upward and thus create inflation. How these factors can influence the employment situation is a more complicated question; but for the reasons mentioned above, any theory should be based on a study of the working of these market mechanisms. It is desirable to make this study as empirical as possible, and this I have tried to do.

Wages and Prices

The relations between the price of labor and other prices must be the first problem to be considered. If Keynes's wage theorem were correct, the price of labor and other prices would move up and down in more or less the same proportion. And, as the quotation from Eichner shows, it was maintained by a Post-Keynesian economist as late as in 1979 that the wage/price relationship is of little or no importance as far as the employment problem is concerned.

That wages and consumer prices have not risen in the same proportion during recent decades is shown clearly in Table 4.2, which covers the seven largest OECD member countries. In the first period wages were rising much more than prices. In the second period the relative differences between the two percentages for each country are smaller. In the next section it will be explained why that is so. Here it may be enough to stress that it cannot be taken for granted that if wages have changed, prices will change in roughly the same proportion.

Real Wages and Productivity

If wages are rising more than consumer prices, real wages are rising. The purchasing power of hourly earnings changes from year to year in a way that can be described as the relation between an

TABLE 4.2: Wages and Consumer Prices; Seven OECD Members, 1962-72 and 1973-79 (percent increase per year)

	1962-72		*1973-79*	
	Wages	*Prices*	*Wages*	*Prices*
United States	4.3	3.3	8.3	8.2
Canada	6.1	3.3	11.2	9.0
Japan	13.4	5.7	13.7	10.4
France	9.0	4.4	14.7	10.2
Germany	7.5	3.2	7.8	5.0
Italy	10.1	4.3	22.4	15.4
United Kingdom	8.2	4.9	16.1	14.8

Note: Wages are hourly earnings in manufacturing.
Source: OECD.

index of wages and an index of consumer prices as this relation alters from year to year.

In Table 4.3 the annual percentage rise of real wages is compared with the annual growth of productivity for the same countries. Productivity is defined as GNP/employment, the gross national product obtained per working hour. The table covers the same countries as Table 4.2 and the same periods.

The table shows that, on the whole, the two growth rates are remarkably close in the first period. In the second period the same is true, with the exception of Italy and the United Kingdom. These two

TABLE 4.3: Real Wages and Productivity; Seven OECD Members, 1962-72 and 1973-79 (percent per year)

	1962-72		1973-79	
	Real Wages	*Productivity*	*Real Wages*	*Productivity*
United States	1.0	1.9	0.1	0.1
Canada	2.7	2.4	2.0	0.3
Japan	7.3	8.7	3.0	3.4
France	4.4	4.6	4.1	2.7
Germany	4.2	4.6	2.7	3.2
Italy	5.6	5.4	6.1	1.6
United Kingdom	3.1	3.0	1.2	0.3

Source: OECD.

countries had fairly high inflation during this period, and it may easily be that under such circumstances the wage rise was ahead of the price rise.

Productivity growth rates are remarkably lower in the second period than in the first. This is because the second period was marked by economic difficulties. A long period of rapid economic growth came to an end in the first half of 1973. At the end of that year the first large oil price rise took place, and it was followed by a period of insecurity and balance-of-payments deficits in many countries. Therefore, rates of investment were low, which tends to dampen productivity growth.

The slow productivity growth during the second period explains why, in Table 4.2, wages did not rise much more than prices during that period. It is worth noting that there was also little productivity growth during the Great Depression of the 1930s, and this may be one of the reasons why Keynes did not find it necessary to undertake a more specific study of the market mechanisms before he concluded that wages and prices were likely to change in roughly the same proportion.

In Table 4.3 the development of real wages is related to productivity growth. The question is what makes productivity grow. In the table productivity is defined as the total result of production (GNP), divided by the quantity of labor. Production is, however, the combined result of the inputs of labor and capital. If productivity is growing, it will usually be because improved methods of production have been introduced. This will, as a rule, be the result of two kinds of efforts. New research and development will have been undertaken and will have led to investment in new types of machinery and other equipment. Both this investment and research and development represent fixed costs, and one of the results may be a reduction of the direct labor costs.

The growing importance of fixed costs is illustrated in Table 3.2 in regard to Italy and the United States. This table shows how difficult it is to get a clear picture of the processes leading to productivity growth. If some inputs have grown fast while others have grown slowly or not at all, how much has each of these factors contributed to the resulting growth of production?

It is not possible to get a precise answer to this question. What one can do is to measure the growth of two of the main inputs, labor and invested capital, at least for some countries. Then one can compare the growth of these two inputs with the growth of production, and finally get a simplified picture of the distribution of the results.

We cannot say whether this distribution is fair or reasonable, since we cannot evaluate the contributions that each of the factors has made to the result. It should not be forgotten that it depends on the market power of business and labor how much each of them is able to obtain.

However, the purpose of the analysis undertaken here is only to judge how the distribution actually taking place influences employment. Once we know how the relations between the prices of products and of labor and capital are developing, we can begin to draw some conclusions regarding the unemployment problem.

In this subsection we have compared the results of production with the input of direct labor and with the income obtained by that labor in the form of real wages. I have made the general remarks above in order to make it clear that the picture is incomplete if it is limited to a comparison of the results with the input of one of the factors of production.

In the following sub-section the input of capital will therefore also be considered. After that the distribution between the factors will be studied in order to make the picture more complete.

Labor, Capital, and Economic Growth

Table 4.4 shows the annual percentage growth of the labor force, of business investment, and of GNP of the seven countries that were covered by Tables 4.2 and 4.3.

In comparing the figures in this table, it should be remembered that while the first and third columns show the annual growth of the labor force and of GNP, the second column does not show the annual growth of capital stock. For each year it shows how much larger gross investment was than the year before. The value of the capital stock cannot be estimated with certainty, and the same is, therefore, true of its growth.

The importance of gross investment is to a large extent due to the fact that it is mainly through new investment that improved methods of production are introduced. Therefore, the figures for the years 1960-73 on the whole show high rates of economic growth for the countries in which investment was growing fast.

In the second period the rates of investment growth and of GNP growth are much lower than in the first period, while the growth of the labor force shows moderate differences between the two periods. This seems to confirm the view that to a very large extent economic growth depends on new investment and on the technical innovations linked to it.

That economic growth could continue after 1973, even in coun-

TABLE 4.4: Growth of Labor, Investment, and GNP; Seven OECD Members, 1960-73 and 1973-78 (annual percent increase)

	1960-73			*1973-78*		
	Labor Force	*Invest-ment*	*GNP*	*Labor Force*	*Invest-ment*	*GNP*
United States	1.9	4.9	4.2	3.0	0.7	2.3
Canada	3.0	6.0	5.1	2.5	2.4	3.0
Japan	1.1	14.3	10.9	0.7	0.0	3.6
France	0.8	7.2	5.9	0.8	0.2	2.6
Germany	0.1	4.2	4.9	0.1	-0.2	1.8
Italy	-0.8	4.6	5.6	0.5	-1.2	1.9
United Kingdom	0.3	4.0	3.3	0.6	3.5	1.1

Sources: Labor force—OECD, *Demographic Trends 1950-1990* (Paris: OECD, 1979), Table IV-1; investment—OECD, *Economic Outlook* no. 26 (1979): Table 6; GNP—OECD.

tries where investment was not increasing, has to do with the fact that investment had reached a high level in 1973 and remained at that level in Japan, while the reduction in Germany and Italy was small. In 1977 gross investment was 30.0 percent of GNP in Japan, 20.9 per cent in Germany, and 19.8 per cent in Italy.[5]

Investment has, thus, been decisive in obtaining economic growth. Much of the investment in recent decades has been in labor-saving machinery. It is a paradox connected with such investment that extra labor is required while the investment is taking place, but the demand for labor will go down when it is finished.

This contrast between the short-term and the long-term effects of such investment may help to explain why the employment situation of OECD members was improving until 1966, as shown in Figure 1.2; after that time unemployment began to increase slowly. It is only after a period with much labor-saving investment that the long-term effect of reducing employment becomes dominant.

Therefore, the first conclusion to be drawn from the analysis undertaken in this chapter is that part of the present unemployment is due to the introduction of more and more labor-saving methods of production. During the second period covered by Table 4.4, the years 1973-78, investment on the whole did not grow, but such investment as there was, was still labor-saving to a high degree.

This raises the question of why there has been such a strong tendency to make the new techniques labor-saving. A comparison between Tables 4.3 and 4.4 can also throw some light on this question. Table 4.3 shows that the revenue of labor grows in more or less the same proportion as productivity. But Table 4.4 seems to indicate that this growth of productivity is due mainly to the increased investment of capital.

This being so, one might expect that capital would gain an increasing part of the total revenue. But this cannot have been the case, since, according to Table 4.3, labor's revenue has grown at the same speed as the total revenue. Capital therefore cannot have obtained an increasing share. It has, in fact, obtained a decreasing share. In addition to the direct labor costs, varying with the quantity of production, the fixed labor costs (salaries) are described in Table 3.2. These costs have been of increasing importance, and therefore what remains as profits has decreased. This means that the rates of return of the capital invested have been declining.

Table 3.2 covers only two countries. The question of the relations between wages and the profits obtained by enterprises is, however, of general interest, since these relations can have a considerable impact on employment. They will be considered in the next subsection.

Profits and Rates of Return

Profits and rates of return have been studied by T. P. Hill.[6] The main conclusions of his study are summarized below as Table 4.5.

The difference between the terms "gross" and "net" in the table is that net profit is the annual profit less depreciation of capital, divided by the total capital invested less accumulated depreciation of former years. From gross profit neither the depreciation of the year in question nor the accumulated depreciation is deducted.

The table shows that during the period covered by the table, profits have represented a declining part of the total value added by production. This corresponds to the conclusion drawn above that direct labor costs seem to have obtained a fairly constant part of the total while fixed costs have absorbed an increasing part. It is obvious that the rates of return capital are bound to go down because the quantity of capital invested has grown faster than the quantity of labor, yet the profits obtained by capital have been a declining part of the total result of production.

It was argued in Chapter 3 that though modern enterprises have often obtained a fairly strong market power as sellers of their products, they have, on the whole, been much weaker in their relations with labor unions. This is partly because, to a fairly high degree, they can get compensation for higher wages through higher prices, and partly because a protracted strike or lockout is dangerous for them. Their large fixed costs must be covered even if there is no production, and the market shares of their competitors in other countries may be increased at their expense.

The analysis undertaken in this chapter has confirmed that while real wages have increased substantially during much of the postwar period, the rates of return of capital have gone down. This means that production has become less remunerative on a rather broad front. That is why this development has contributed to the increase of unemployment that has made the employment problem so serious.

When profitability is declining, an enterprise can defend itself in two ways. It can stop production in the parts of the business where profitability is particularly low, even negative. Or it can change the methods of production where this can reduce costs perceptibly—for instance, by introducing labor-saving techniques. In both cases employment will be reduced, which clearly demonstrates the paradoxical situation of labor in the modern society.

We have seen that, on the whole, labor unions have been in a strong position in their relations with the business sector. The real prices of labor have increased compared with the returns on capital.

TABLE 4.5: Profit Shares and Rates of Return, Trend Percentage Rates of Change; Selected Countries, 1958-76

	Manufacturing				*Industry plus Transport*			
	Profit Share P/Y (%)		*Rate of Return* P/K (%)		*Profit Share* P/T (%)		*Rate of Return* P/K (%)	
Country	*Gross*	Net	*Gross*	Net	*Gross*	Net	*Gross*	Net
Canada	-0.4	-0.8	-1.1	-1.4	-0.1	-0.4	-0.6	-1.1
United States[a]	-0.1	-0.3	-0.4	-0.7	-0.7	-1.1	-1.1	-2.0
Japan[b]	-0.9	-1.7	-1.8	-3.9	-0.8	-1.6	-0.2	-2.4
Australia[b]	-0.5	-0.9	—	—	-0.1	-0.4	—	—
Denmark[b]	-1.5	—	—	—	-0.5	—	—	—
Germany	-2.3	-4.2	-3.1	-4.6	-0.7	-1.1	-1.9	-2.9
Italy[c]	-2.0	-2.5	-1.7	-2.0	-1.8	-2.1	-1.2	-1.8
Netherlands	-1.1	-1.1	—	—	-0.9	-1.3	—	—
Sweden	-0.1	-0.4	-0.6	-0.9	-1.4	-2.9	-2.3	-4.1
United Kingdom	-3.4	-6.2	-5.4	-8.5	-0.6	-2.2	-1.9	-4.1

Note: These figures show the trend percentage changes from year to year in the share, or rate of return, not the number of percentage points by which the share or rate of return changes. For example, a fall from 20 percent to 19 percent represents a decline of 5 percent (1/20x100) in the table, not 1 percent.

[a] The U.S. data for industry plus transport also include distribution and miscellaneous services.

[b] The trends for these countries cover 1958-75.

[c] The trends for Italy cover 1955-72.

Y = Total value added.

K = Capital.

P = Profits.

— = Not available.

Source: T. P. Hill, *Profits and Rates of Return* (Paris: OECD 1979), p. 23.

But, as indicated in the section "Historical Background," there is a particular vulnerability on the part of those who have to sell their labor in order to gain a living. The paradox of the modern labor market is that the stronger the unions are, the greater the risk that a substantial number of their members become unemployed.

So far we have looked at a national labor market as one single market. There may, however, be substantial differences between the functioning of the mechanisms in various parts of the economy, and these differences can influence the employment situation in different ways. It is, therefore, necessary to study the consequences of these differences.

Market Power and Techniques

In the "Competing and Sheltered Sectors" in Chapter 3, a distinction was made between what have been called the sheltered and the competing sectors. The difference is that the latter is exposed to foreign competition, while the former is not. As a consequence prices have been rising more in the sheltered than in the competing sector, as shown in Table 3.1. These differences were very marked during the 1950s and the 1960s. They were somewhat less spectacular during the 1970s, because during that time inflation became fairly strong in the international community as a whole. There was, nevertheless, a clear difference between the two rates of price rise, except in the United States, where the falling value of the dollar led to rapidly rising import and export prices.

The question is how these variations in price behavior have influenced production in the two sectors. This is shown in Table 4.6 for the same countries that were covered by Table 3.1.

Obviously the competing sector was in the weaker position of the two. Its production grew more slowly than that of the sheltered sector except in the Netherlands, which was in a strong competitive position in these years. As a result its currency gradually appreciated. The competing sector was particularly weak in the United Kingdom and the United States. In contrast with the Netherlands, these two countries were in a weak competitive position that gradually led to a depreciation of their currencies.

As mentioned earlier, enterprises in a weak position can defend themselves in two ways. They can reduce production where it is unremunerative or they can change their methods of production. No doubt many enterprises in the competing sector have reduced production, with the result that the sector as a whole has had relatively low growth rates.

TABLE 4.6: Production and Employment; Selected Countries, 1970-75

	Production 1975 (1970 = 100)		*Employment (Million)*			
			1970	*1975*	*1970*	*1975*
	C	S	C		S	
Austria	115	124	1.5	1.3	1.5	1.7
Belgium	117	122	1.4	1.3	2.2	2.4
France	117	124	8.8	8.3	11.6	12.5
Netherlands	119	115	1.6	1.4	3.0	3.1
United Kingdom	100	111	9.7	8.7	14.7	15.9
United States	106	116	23.4	22.5	50.9	57.9

C = Competing.

S = Sheltered.

Sources: National Accounts of OECD Countries, 1960-77, various tables; International Labour Organization, *Yearbook of Labour Statistics* (Geneva: ILO, 1976), various tables.

It is, however, particularly through improved methods of production that the competing sector has tried to remedy the difficult position in which it has been placed because its prices have been rising much less than those of the sheltered sector, while wages have been rising at approximately the same pace in the two sectors. It was shown in Table 3.1 that productivity increased substantially faster in the competing than in the sheltered sector. As mentioned above, in recent decades new methods of production have to a very large extent meant more labor-saving methods.

It is, therefore, not surprising that Table 4.6 shows declining employment in the competing sector in all six countries concerned. Both a reduction of production and the introduction of labor-saving techniques work in that direction. It is part of the causation of the present unemployment problem that the parts of the economy that are in a weak position are bound to accept the same wage rises as the parts that are in a stronger position. Table 4.6 shows that the sheltered sector represents the larger part of the labor force in all six countries. It therefore has a strong position in wage negotiations. And, as mentioned below, an important part of the competing sector has a similar position.

This has to do with the fact, mentioned in Chapter 3, that it is an oversimplification to distinguish between the competing and the sheltered sectors in the way it is done in the study by Gösta Edgren et al. (see Chapter 3). An important part of what is called the competing sector consists of large enterprises that have a considerable degree of market power. On the other hand, some parts of the sheltered sector are exposed to competition that can be serious. For instance, traditional retail shops are threatened by supermarkets and some handicrafts are threatened by modern industry.

It will, therefore, be more generally useful to distinguish between the enterprises that have a relatively strong market power and those that are in a weak position because they are exposed to strong competition, whether it stems from foreign trade or from the home market. These two types of situations are depicted in Figure 4.1, where the demand curves (D) describe the relations between the prices charged and the quantities that can be sold.

The difference in the slope of the demand curve (D) is decisive. Enterprises of type A are exposed to strong competition. If the price (p) is raised only slightly, the quantity sold (x) will be reduced substantially. Enterprises of type B are in a stronger position. They can raise prices considerably and yet experience only a modest reduction of sales.

Enterprises of type A, then, have a weak market power. They are

FIGURE 4.1: Two Degrees of Market Power

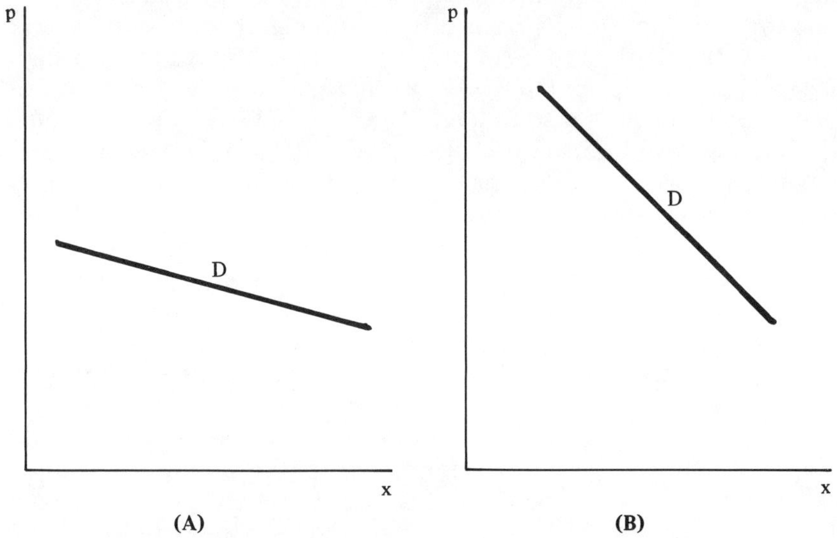

Source: Constructed by the author.

not far from the situation in a market with free or perfect competition, where the demand curve would be horizontal (that is, the price would be of a given magnitude on which the individual producer had no influence. Enterprises of type B have much more market power. They can, therefore, get more compensation by raising their prices if wages are increasing. In practice there are many different degrees of market power, but there has been a growing degree of concentration, and therefore also of market power, in many branches of industry.

There is another difference between enterprises that is important in the situation discussed here. Enterprises that have a labor-intensive kind of production will be affected more by a wage rise than those that have more capital-intensive types of production. Their reactions to a wage rise can, therefore, be expected to be different. Enterprises of type B will raise their prices relatively more, especially if their production is of the labor-intensive type. Those of type A are in a more difficult position. If they raise their prices only moderately, sales will go down to an appreciable extent. They will be hit particularly hard if their production is labor-intensive.

These two kinds of differences between enterprises can be shown in combination, as is done in Figure 4.2

Historically the trend has been from Type 1 through Types 2 and 3 toward Type 4. Enterprises have become larger, their methods of

FIGURE 4.2: Four Types of Enterprises

Market Power \ Techniques	Labor-Intensive	Capital-Intensive
Weak	1	2
Strong	3	4

Source: Constructed by the author.

production have become more capital-intensive, and they have acquired more market power because of their size or because they have joined other enterprises in cartels.

This general movement, combined with rising wages, has created unemployment in various ways. Many small enterprises of Type 1 have disappeared. Small farmers have given up and sold their land to larger farmers. Shopkeepers have given up, being defeated by supermarkets, and artisans have been replaced by factories.

It was mentioned in the section "Historical Background" that those who have to sell their labor are in a vulnerable position because they may become unemployed. It should be added that small entrepreneurs run the same risk of not being able to earn a living. This is one of the causes of the increasing unemployment of recent decades. Other enterprises may react to rising wages by becoming more capital-intensive, thus moving toward Type 2 or 4. That of course also creates unemployment.

When enterprises get more market power, moving toward Type 3 or 4, their own risks are reduced. But if they react to increasing wages by raising their prices, they must accept a certain reduction of their sales, as shown in Figure 4.1.B.

The analysis undertaken so far points to the conclusion that after a general wage rise some prices will be raised very little, others somewhat more; but since all transactions will now take place at higher wages and prices, the amount of money circulating in the country must be allowed to increase somewhat. Even if that is allowed, some unemployment will result if the wage rise is of such a magnitude that profits continue their long-term decline, as shown in

Table 4.5. It is because of this decline that production is becoming unremunerative in more and more cases, especially in enterprises of Types 1 and 2.

Transnational Price Fixing

So far it has tacitly been assumed that the various processes discussed take place in one country. To an increasing extent, however, prices are fixed in one country while the goods in question are sold in other countries. This can have a disturbing effect on employment in two radically different cases.

Prices can be fixed at a particularly low level for some time because the producers are trying through a price war to destroy their competitors in the countries where the goods are sold. If they succeed, there will be some unemployment in these countries, and after that prices may be raised. A similar price war may, or course, take place within a single country, but in that case the authorities may be able to intervene. Whether they can intervene in the case of a transnational price war depends on the international rules concerning trade policy.

The other extreme is those cases where prices are high because of the market power of the enterprises that sell their products in foreign countries. Export cartels can have this effect, but there can also be cases where a single enterprise is strong enough to charge such prices. Whether this can influence employment naturally depends on the nature of the goods concerned. If they are raw materials or semimanufactured articles, a price rise means higher costs of production, which can lead to unemployment until the whole economic system has been adjusted to the new situation.

A case in point is the price policy of the oil cartel, OPEC. The price rises since 1973 have led to a number of changes in the oil-importing countries. There are fewer cars than there otherwise would have been, and activities requiring much energy have been reduced. More generally, the sharp deterioration of the balances of payments of many countries has forced governments to pursue restrictive policies that have reduced employment.

On the other hand, the oil price rises have furthered such activities as oil drilling, the development of new sources of energy and of machinery and installations that require less energy, and so on. The trouble is, however, that all the changes mentioned are dependent on the capacity of the economic systems to adjust to new situations. This general problem will be dealt with in Chapter 6. Here it may be said in conclusion that changes in transnational price fixing are less disturbing if they take place gradually, over a longer period, than they did in the case of oil. The adjustment processes take time.

Equalization of Wages

As shown in Table 4.1, a national labor force is composed of many different types of labor, and therefore there are many levels of wages and salaries. There has been a tendency on the part of labor unions to work toward an equalization of wages by asking for specific increases favoring those at the lowest wage levels. The question is how this can influence employment.

In modern societies there may be a long-term trend toward an equalization of qualifications. The general level of education is rising, and many of the simplest tasks are being taken over by machines. If the development of the various categories of wages proceeds in conformity with this development of qualifications, no serious problems of adjustment should arise.

Problems do arise, however, if wages for the lower ranks of the labor force are pushed upward at a time when no corresponding increase in their economic value has taken place. The result may, in fact, be more unemployment among exactly those groups of workers who were to be helped. There are two reasons for this.

One is that the work in question may not be done at all if its price is raised. The number of house maids has gone down drastically, and in supermarkets the customers must do part of the work that was done by the shopkeeper and his assistants in traditional retail trade. Many articles that used to be repaired are now thrown away. The other reason why some of the people belonging to the lowest-paying categories of the labor force can lose their jobs if their wages are raised, has to do with the quality of their work, which may not be high enough to justify the wage increase.

This can be illustrated by a simple example. Let there be two categories of workers, a and b. Those of category a have the higher wages because they can do things that those of category b cannot do. Or they can do the same things better than those of category b. If the wages of category b are raised, coming closer to those of category a, some employers who used to employ b workers because they were cheap will now prefer a workers because the difference in price has become very small compared with the difference in quality.

This will have two consequences. One is that there will be unemployment among b workers. The other is that the increasing demand for a workers will tend gradually to cause a rise in their wages too. In this way the wage rise tends to spread upward through the labor force. As a result, the general wage level will be raised somewhat, and after a while the difference between the wages of categories a and b will be almost the same as before the rise of b wages.

I have tried to follow the development of the Danish labor market through a number of years in order to study this particular problem. My general impression has been that after a decision to raise some of the lowest wages, there has been more wage drift in the categories representing higher levels. After a few years the various wage differentials are approximately the same as before the decision was made.

It must be added, though, that there has been a long-term trend toward an equalization of wages, but this has had to do with the long-term trend toward an equalization of qualifications. It seems, in particular, that many of the so-called unskilled workers have now acquired skills that bring the quality of their labor closer to that of the skilled workers.

Capital Markets

The study of the product and labor markets undertaken above has revealed two tendencies that have to do with the capital markets. One is that labor has increasingly been replaced by capital through investment in labor-saving machinery. The other is that the rates of return of the capital invested have been falling, as shown in Table 4.5.

Between them these two tendencies seem to raise the following question: Why do enterprises continue to invest as much as they have done when the rates of return of the capital invested have been going down through a large part of the postwar period? The answer to that question can to a large extent be found in the development of the capital markets, which was described in Chapter 3. Because of inflation, the real rates of interest have been going down even more than the rates of return. In many cases the real rates of interest on loans have become negative.

If the real price of capital is negative, even rather poor investments may appear to be remunerative. If the rate of return of an investment is around zero, it will nevertheless be profitable to make the investment if capital can be borrowed at -3 percent per year.

It should be added that in the tax legislation, rules regarding depreciation are often laid down that are intended to favor investment. It is, of course, hoped that this may lead to a higher rate of employment and, as mentioned above, this may happen on a short view. However, the more permanent result will often be a reduction of employment because labor-saving techniques are furthered. In politics it is always tempting to pay most attention to the short-term effects.

There has been a widespread inclination to believe that investment depends primarily on prosperity and economic growth. If an economy is prosperous and profits are high, there will be much investment. In a period of difficulties and low rates of return, investment will be discouraged. Table 4.4 would seem to support this kind of reasoning. Investment was growing quickly during 1960-73, when there was rapid economic growth. It was stagnating, on the whole, during the difficult years after 1973.

It should, however, be remembered that business investment can have two different purposes. One is to maintain or increase capacity; the other is to make the methods of production more profitable. We may call them capacity investment and profitability investment, respectively.

It is capacity investment if, for example, a firm in the textile industry replaces old machinery and perhaps buys more machinery so that it can produce as much cloth as before or even more. And it is profitability investment if the firm buys new machinery that will enable it to produce cloth at lower costs than before.

The same investment can be both a capacity and a profitability investment. It is important to note, however, that though the rates of economic growth have been low since 1973, the rates of inflation have been high, so that borrowed capital can be repaid with money that is worth much less than the money borrowed. Therefore, the real rates of interest have been negative for many investors, making it profitable to replace labor by capital. As a consequence, it is likely that an increasing part of total investment after 1973 has been profitability investment, replacing labor by capital and thus creating more unemployment in the long run.

If we examine the seven countries covered by Table 4.4 as a whole, we find that investment has not been reduced since 1973. It has continued at the fairly high level it has reached in 1973, and since economic growth has been slow, there is reason to believe that capacity investment has played a modest role.

It is worth noting that profitability investment can continue even if the rates of return of existing capital are low. If new capital can be invested in more profitable ways, the average rates of return should become higher. It may, therefore, be expected that much labor-saving capital investment will continue to be made as long as the rates of inflation remain high. The fact that the international capital markets have been fairly well supplied with liquidity favors such investment.

It is important to note that one of the consequences of high rates of inflation through a period of years will be a continued tendency to replace labor by capital because there is no way to prevent the real rates of interest from remaining negative for many investors.

It is no longer believed that through demand management we can choose between unemployment and inflation. We now have both, and a paradoxical consequence of the new situation is that inflation tends to further unemployment.

The Public Sector

Because of the large budgets of central and local governments in all modern societies, the political authorities have the responsibility for the volume of total demand. If wages increase at the expense of profits, the direct consequence may be a higher level of consumption without a corresponding reduction of investment, because the capacity to produce consumer goods may have to be increased. But this raises the question of whether the national economy can afford this expansion. Will not imports be too large? Will it not be necessary to increase taxation or reduce public expenditure?

The section "Demand Management" in Chapter 3 showed how difficult it has become to regulate total demand through fiscal and monetary policies. If demand is reduced, there will be more unemployment and the rates of inflation will not be lowered perceptibly. If expansionary policies are pursued, there will be more inflation, and the employment situation may improve only temporarily. What was said in the previous section about the long-term effects of inflation seems to support this reasoning.

This leads to the conclusion that from the point of view of internal stability, it is desirable not to change fiscal and monetary policies frequently. As long as market mechanisms function as they do today, the negative consequences of both types of policy change tend to be large compared with the positive effects.

To this must be added that the oil prices of recent years have created balance-of-payments deficits in a large number of oil-importing countries. Many governments have therefore been constrained by the balance-of-payments position to pursue restrictive policies. This is one of the reasons why the rates of unemployment are so high. Because of the weak self-adjusting forces of modern economies, we have the paradoxical situation that the necessity of economizing makes us waste an important resource: labor.

There is another paradox in the present situation. Restrictive policies have the purpose of reducing imports, but most of the imports of Western countries come from other Western countries. They therefore reduce the exports of these countries, and the net result is only a modest influence on the balance of payments of the West as a whole.

There will, however, be more unemployment in many countries because of these policies, and what has been said about the West can be extended to comprise all the oil-importing countries and some of the oil exporters. The outlook today is that a small group of oil-exporting countries will have a large balance-of-payments surplus for many years to come. It follows that the rest of the world will have a corresponding deficit.

There might be less unemployment in the world as a whole if all the countries involved were able to coordinate their policies and decide how this deficit should be distributed among them, but that is hardly possible. International cooperation has not yet been developed to such a high degree. We are therefore left with a situation where the main responsibility remains with the individual governments and parliaments. This being so, the waste of human resources through unemployment will continue until the capacity of our economies to adjust to changing circumstances has been increased to a substantial degree. That will be the main subject of Chapter 6.

International Relations

In the section "International Inflation Problems" of Chapter 3, it was discussed how inflation can be transmitted from countries with high rates of inflation to countries with more stable prices. There will be a certain transmission of unemployment in the opposite direction. The countries that can keep their price levels nearly constant while prices are rising in other countries, will become more competitive, thus stimulating their exports to the countries with inflation. As a consequence, unemployment will go down in the former countries while it will increase in the latter. The interdependence of countries has been of growing importance in this field, as in others during the postwar period, because international trade has become more free.

As the transmission of inflation can be counteracted by changes in the exchange rates corresponding to the changes in price levels, the same will be true of the transmission of unemployment. In both cases it is, however, a condition of success that the devaluation in countries with high rates of inflation is followed by measures to achieve greater price stability.

In recent years countries with unemployment and other difficulties in the business sector have often tried to alleviate the situation by restricting imports, thus protecting their own enterprises against foreign competition. This has been difficult because the rules of GATT and other international organizations have for many years aimed at liberalizing foreign trade.

The "new protectionism" of recent years has, therefore, tried to avoid direct import restrictions and replace them by indirect methods. Sometimes a country has tried to persuade other countries deliberately to reduce their exports to it. Or governments have subsidized national enterprises so that they can lower their prices and become more competitive.

Whatever the methods may be, the direct result will be a transmission of unemployment to other countries. Internationally, this is no solution to the problem. But even for the country trying to export its difficulties in that way, it will often mean only a postponement of needed adjustments. This will particularly be the case if a number of countries are taking such measures at the same time in order to avoid the liquidation of enterprises. The result may be that too much production capacity is maintained in the world as a whole, and therefore it is unavoidable that some enterprises will close down.

In this, as in other cases discussed in this chapter, the major part of the problem stems from the fact that modern market systems tend to create unemployment as well as inflation.

Reactions to Change

In the first part of this chapter we have considered the working of the economic systems of modern societies as it influences the employment situation. In this second part we shall study how these systems react to certain changes in the external circumstances under which they have to work. Three such changes will be considered: technological change, changes in the international division of labor, and changes in the rates of economic growth.

Other changes might also have been discussed, such as the growing concern about the environment or, in a more general way, changes in political attitudes. The problems to be studied are, roughly speaking, the same regardless of the nature of the changes concerned. In all conceivable cases there are two questions to be raised: How does the change influence the economic systems, and employment in particular? How do the economic systems react to the change to which they have been exposed?

It is, therefore, preferable to concentrate on changes whose effects on the systems can be defined in a relatively precise way.

Technological Change

It has been discussed in economic literature whether technological change is an exogenous factor that influences the economic system from the outside, or whether it is an endogenous factor, originating within the system itself.

The answer to that question is that it can be either, and often it will be a mixture of the two. New technologies concerning oil drilling are being developed because of the oil price rises of recent years. They can, therefore, be said to originate within the system. The same is true of many of the labor-saving innovations referred to earlier in this chapter. But nuclear energy would never have become a possibility had certain developments within theoretical physics not taken place.

Whether a technological innovation has its origins wholly or partly, or not at all, within the economic system, it is, however, something new which may influence the system. In principle, technological innovations can have three different kinds of purposes: to create new products, to improve existing products, or to make products cheaper. There are no sharp distinctions among these purposes. If the quality of a product is changed substantially, is it still the same product, or is it a new one? Often the process of production can be made cheaper only if changes in its quality are accepted.

In any case, the innovations will open up new possibilities of production and will expose some existing producers to new competition. This is partly why modern enterprises find it necessary to have large research and development departments: so that they can make innovations and react quickly to innovations made by others.

Whether the innovation consists of a new product or a new method of production, one of the results may be that a certain need can be satisfied with less labor than before. This has been one of the factors leading to unemployment in modern societies. Also, in earlier times many of the most important innovations were labor-saving. Manpower has been replaced by horsepower, water mills, windmills, steam engines, and so on.

A distinction should, however, be made between the direct and the indirect consequences of an innovation. It is particularly important to be aware of this concerning labor-saving innovations. The direct consequence of such an innovation is that less time is required to perform a certain task, but this is only the direct consequence. Since human needs are nearly endless, the indirect consequences of a labor-saving innovation will often include new activities that require a substantial amount of work.

Sometimes these new activities represent an extension of the older activities that were made easier by the innovation. The automobile is a labor-saving device, but because it is so easy to travel by car, people today are, on the average, driving many more hours per year than people did two generations ago. To this may be added the work required to produce and repair automobiles, as well as the roads and bridges on which they are driven. Another example is the airplane. This is also a labor-saving device, but it has enabled people to move over long distances to an extent that was inconceivable a few decades ago.

It is worth noting that the direct consequences of an innovation are felt immediately, at least to some extent. The indirect consequences often appear only over a long period, and they may create jobs in fields other than those where the direct consequences make jobs disappear.

There are other technological changes that are not labor-saving and where the direct consequence is the creation of new jobs. Television is an innovation that has given rise to a new industry and to many activities of various kinds. To what extent this represents a net addition to the demand for labor, nobody can tell. A new possibility of spending money must always compete with the possibilities already existing. But, as in the case of a labor-saving device, people can react to a new, interesting product in two ways. They can reduce their consumption of other goods in order to be able to buy the new product. Or they can try to increase their income in order to be able to buy the new product without reducing their consumption of other goods.

Many married women have entered the labor market in recent years, and one of the reasons is that their families would like to increase their incomes because there are so many new things that it would be desirable to have—a car, a television set, or a pleasure boat, for instance. Or the family might want to travel to other countries.

That many women have entered the labor market in this way throws some light on one aspect of the present employment problem. Technological innovations not only can raise or reduce the demand for labor in various fields; they also can influence the supply of labor—for example, increasing it by offering new possibilities of consumption.

This new tendency for married women to enter the labor market has had some indirect consequences. There has been an increasing demand for nursery schools because often both parents are away from home for several hours each day. And a great deal of labor-saving kitchen equipment has been invented in order to save time for working women.

There is one aspect of modern technological development that should be considered before an effort is made to draw some general conclusions. The so-called electronics revolution is unique in more than one respect. Innovations have taken place at an unusual speed over a number of years, and this is expected to continue for many years to come. And at a time when productivity in general is growing slowly, as shown in Table 4.3, it is growing surprisingly fast in the electronics industry.

A special issue of the American journal *Science* was devoted to the electronics revolution.[7] The following sentences from the lead article give an indication of the essence of the review undertaken in a number of articles:

> The dynamism of electronics is in sharp contrast to the slow-moving, static or deteriorating situations encountered in energy, food and nutrition, and materials. The days of easy exploitation of natural resources have passed, and adjustments to scarcities and to the use of substitutes will be slow and difficult.
>
> . . .
>
> As the vigor of the industrial revolution fades, the electronics revolution will provide impetus for the reshaping of society in new directions.[8]

There are two aspects of the electronics revolution that should be stressed. It makes information of all kinds easily available to a degree unheard-of earlier. And it furthers automation in industry and services through the feeding of information into machines and thereby steering the production processes.

Opinions vary regarding the possible consequences of this new development. There are four changes in particular that might influence the employment situation, and that should therefore be taken into account in a study of the unemployment problem. They can be described briefly in the following way:

1. Because of increased automation, there may be a drastic reduction of the demand for some kinds of labor. This reduction may occur in industry as well as in banking and other private service activities, and finally in the public sector.
2. On the other hand, electronics may open up many new possibilities, as the automobile and television have. There may, therefore, be an increased demand for labor in a number of fields. But to a large extent this demand will be for labor with qualifications other than those of the people who become redundant because of automation.
3. It may be that small enterprises will have new possibilities to compete with larger enterprises because small-scale equipment will be furnished

by the electronics industry. As a consequence, the tendency for enterprises to become larger and larger may be interrupted in some branches.
4. The central part of the hardware used in electronic processes has been drastically reduced in size, compared with its capacity. Therefore, at least some parts of the electronics industry may prove to be unique as regards their needs for the factors of production. As mentioned earlier, it has been characteristic of postwar technological development that production has become labor-saving while requiring more capital. But certain parts of the electronics industry may prove to be both labor- and capital-saving at the same time.

It will be discussed below, in the section regarding the rates of economic growth, how modern societies are likely to go through a period when capital investment cannot increase as it did in the years up to 1973. It will, therefore, be helpful if capital needs are reduced in some fields, simply because of the nature of the new processes.

Looking back at the various types of technological change, it should be possible to get an impression of the kind of impact they are likely to exert on modern economies, especially as regards employment. And then we can look at the ways in which these economies react to such influences.

These influences can be grouped in four categories:

1. There will be a reduced demand for some kinds of labor, perhaps on a large scale in some cases.
2. There will be an increased demand for some other kinds of labor.
3. It is possible that the net result will be a reduction of the total demand for labor.
4. There would be an increased demand for capital in many fields if economic growth should resume its former role, and thereby counteract the growth of unemployment to some extent. Capital saving because of the electronics revolution may not be important for some years to come.

How do modern economies react to these changes? It is likely that the first category of changes will lead to more unemployment as it has until now. Those who become redundant in banking or in some parts of the public sector will not easily be absorbed elsewhere. Wages and salaries will not be reduced, as they would have been in former times, and those who lose their jobs often will not be qualified to take the jobs that become vacant in other parts of the economy.

For the same reason these jobs will, in many cases, not be easy to fill. The increased demand for some kinds of labor, mentioned in the second category, may lead to higher wages or salaries because the supply is not increasing fast enough. Only gradually will a sufficient number of people be trained for the new jobs created by technological change.

It is a characteristic feature of modern societies that there can be unemployment and shortage of labor at the same time. The mobility of a modern labor force is limited, partly because it is composed of many specialized groups. This is particularly unfortunate in an age dominated by rapid technological change, creating a special need for moving people from those parts of the labor market where demand is falling to those parts where it is rising.

With the present functioning of the market mechanisms, the result is likely to be both more unemployment and more inflation. There will be more unemployment in the parts of the labor market where demand is falling. And in the parts where demand is rising, higher wages will make a contribution to the process of inflation.

There will be especially high unemployment if, as mentioned in the third category, the net result of the technological changes is a reduction in the total demand for labor. The fact that most modern techniques are capital-intensive has led to the opinion, sometimes also advanced by economists, that we can come back to full employment only through a new process of rapid, capital-intensive economic growth.

I think this is unrealistic. The rapid economic growth during the years from 1960 to 1973 led to increasing rates of inflation, and also to increasing pollution and energy consumption. The international monetary system, based on fixed but adjustable rates of exchange, was gradually breaking down and the employment situation was improving only during the first part of the period.

A new period of rapid economic growth of the old type will be even more difficult to endure than the previous such period because energy prices are now much higher, because many countries now have balance-of-payments difficulties, and because inflation and unemployment have now been built into the system to a degree unknown before 1973.

It follows that we are not likely to get back to full employment in the foreseeable future with the present working of the market mechanisms and with continued technological change of the types dominating in recent years. Substantial new changes will, therefore, be needed. I will come back to these questions in Chapter 6.

The International Division of Labor

One of the most important changes to which Western economies will be exposed in the years to come is the growing competition from the manufacturing industry of the South. This development has been described in the report of the Independent Commission on International Development Issues under the chairmanship of Willy Brandt.[9]

The report states that while the developing countries had around 7 percent of world manufacturing in the 1960s, their share had risen to 9 percent in 1977. And a growing part of the total imports of the West from non-OPEC developing countries consists of manufactures. In 1976 it was about 40 percent in the United States, 24 percent in Japan, and 29 percent in the EEC.

These percentages are likely to rise further in the future. The less-developed regions of the world have less than half as much agricultural land per capita as the more developed regions, and this difference is bound to grow in the decades to come because of the rapid population growth in the South. According to the UN projections of 1978, the world's population can be expected to grow as shown below.

	1980 (million)	*2000 (million)*	*Increase (million)*
More-developed regions	1,131	1,272	141
Less-developed regions	3,284	4,926	1,642
Total	4,415	6,198	1,783

More than 90 percent of the population growth during these 20 years can, then, be expected to take place in the South. This means that there will be increasing pressure on the land, and people will move out of agriculture on a large scale, as they have already done in the North. It follows that the comparative advantage of the South will not be in agriculture. It will be in industry, where a rapidly growing, cheap labor force will be available. And the quality of this labor force is gradually improving because of rising educational standards.

Multinational corporations that have their headquarters in the West are transferring increasing parts of their production to the South, where labor is cheap and markets are growing. This is a natural development, and it is desirable from a global point of view. But it means that the labor force of the West is meeting competition from the large labor force of the South, both in the markets of the West and in those of the South.

According to the Brandt report, 32 percent of the manufactured exports of the South went to other countries in the South in 1976, and it was a growing percentage. The growing role of the South in the world economy will be discussed more fully in Chapter 5. Here it should be stressed that the industrialization of the South is influencing the economies of the West in two different ways.

Industry in the South is taking over an increasing part of some of the markets for manufactures. But the industrialization of the South has been made possible by increasing imports of machinery and other production equipment from the North. And these imports have come from the West much more than from the East.

What is developing is, therefore, a new international division of labor. The West is losing market shares in some of the most labor-intensive branches of industry, but at the same time it is finding larger markets for some of its manufactured products, mainly machinery but also high-quality consumer goods for the wealthy minority groups in the poor countries.

The impact of these changes is, therefore, of the same nature as the impact of technological change discussed in the previous section. Demand will be declining for some relatively simple types of labor and it will be increasing for more sophisticated work.

This, at least, is the picture one gets in the years around 1980. It can, however, be expected that during the next few decades the South will become a competitor on more equal terms in its relations with the West. Already countries like South Korea and Brazil are taking over small but growing shares of the relatively sophisticated shipbuilding industry. But the more complicated types of ships are still built in the West.

The conclusion of this short survey is that the West must be prepared for a gradual transformation of the international division of labor. The question, therefore, is whether its market mechanisms can be made flexible enough so that the adaptation to change that will be required can be accomplished without increasing unemployment in some parts of the labor market.

Until now a number of Western countries have tried to defend themselves against competition from the South through various forms of protection. This is, however, only postponing the adaptation that will become necessary. In this case, as in the case of technological change discussed above, there will be a growing need to improve the methods of adjustment of modern economies. As already mentioned, this will be the main subject of Chapter 6.

Changing Rates of Economic Growth

For the OECD area as a whole, real GNP was growing by 5.5 percent per year from 1959-60 to 1972-73.[10] In 1979 the most likely growth for the period 1975-2000 was estimated to be 3.4 percent per year.[11] As mentioned in the section "Technological Change," there are two reasons why rapid growth, as experienced during the years up to 1973, cannot be expected to be possible in the future.

One is that the process of rapid economic growth had a number of unfortunate consequences that would be unacceptable in the long run: growing rates of inflation, increasing pollution, rapidly increasing energy consumption, and a gradual breakdown of the international monetary system. Even the employment situation began to deteriorate during the latter part of the period of rapid economic growth, as can be seen from Figure 1.2. The other reason is the changed energy situation. The higher oil prices represent a burden on all oil-importing countries, and balance-of-payments deficits are forcing them to adopt cautious economic policies.

To this can be added that an increasing part of the investment taking place has been devoted to oil drilling and to other efforts to develop energy sources other than oil from OPEC countries. A certain amount of investment will, therefore, create less economic growth than would otherwise have been the case.

The question now is how the economic systems of modern societies are reacting to this radical change in their prospects for economic growth. And it is particularly important to consider the consequences of this pattern as regards employment. As can be seen from Table 4.4, the reaction during the first part of the new era has been low rates of investment and low rates of economic growth. At the same time the rates of unemployment have been high. This means that the reaction so far has not been successful.

During the first years after the turning point in 1973, the opinion was often expressed that we must speed up economic growth in order to get back to full employment. But now it is gradually being recognized that rapid economic growth is not likely to be resumed during the next couple of decades. The apparently easy solution of just pushing demand so that growth rates can be high is, therefore, no real solution.

This does not mean that it is impossible to get back to full employment. The question is in which ways the working of the economic systems has to be changed in order to make that possible. Like other policy problems, this question will be discussed in Chapter 6. It may, however, be useful in this concluding part of a chapter on unemployment to make some general remarks about the relations between employment and economic growth. That should throw some light on the question of what went wrong during the 1970s.

There will always be some frictional unemployment because those who lose their jobs cannot in all cases immediately find the vacant jobs that exist. Mobility is never perfect. But apart from that, full employment can be maintained at any rate of economic growth. If the labor force grows by 1 percent per year and the annual growth of productivity per worker is 2 percent, full employment can be maintained with an economic growth of 3.02 percent per year (1.01 x 1.02 = 1.032). If the annual productivity growth is 4 percent, an overall growth rate of 5.04 per cent will be required.

It follows that if lower overall growth rates have to be accepted, lower rates of growth of productivity per worker also must be accepted if full employment is to be maintained. This is an important point. An overall growth rate of 3.02 percent can be obtained in two different ways. It can, as indicated above, be obtained with an annual growth of employment of 1 percent and a growth of productivity per worker of 2 percent. It can, however, also be obtained through an annual growth of productivity per worker of 3.02 percent and no growth of employment.

If this were to happen—that is, if employment remained constant while the labor force available was increasing by 1 percent per year—a growing part of that labor force would become unemployed.

In a more general way, if the productivity per worker continues to grow so fast that the overall growth that is possible can allow only a declining part of the available labor force to be employed, there will be growing rates of unemployment. This is exactly what has happened. It can be seen from Table 4.2 that productivity growth rates were high during the years until 1973, and even after the turning point they were kept fairly high in some of the countries though the overall growth rates were low.

Other things being equal, productivity growth rates will be high when much capital is invested per worker. The methods of production will then be capital-intensive, and that is what they have become more and more during the 1960s and 1970s. As mentioned earlier, such methods create some demand for labor while the investment needed is carried through, but the long-term effect is in the opposite direction.

Capital-intensive methods of production will be applied as long as the real price of labor is high compared with the real price of capital. And, as already mentioned, the real price of capital has increasingly become negative because of inflation. As long as this is true, any price of labor will be high compared with the real price of capital.

Full employment could be obtained even with low overall rates of economic growth if the methods of production were sufficiently labor-intensive so that there was more employment for each percent the total GNP was able to grow.

We must, therefore, conclude that the price mechanisms have not been able to adjust the economic systems to the lower rates of growth we now have to accept. And inflation is a major cause of this lack of adjustment.

NOTES

1. John M. Keynes, *The General Theory of Employment, Interest and Money* (London: MacMillan & Co. 1936), p. 269.
2. John Hicks, *The Crisis in Keynesian Economics* (Oxford: Basil Blackwell, 1975), pp. 59-60.
3. R. F. Harrod, *John Maynard Keynes* (Harmondsworth: Penguin Books, 1972), p. 474.
4. Alfred S. Eichner, "A Post Keynesian Short-Period Model," *Journal of Post-Keynesian Economics* 1, no. 4 (1979): 40.
5. *OECD Observer* no. 97 (Mar. 1979): 22.
6. T. P. Hill, *Profits and Rates of Return* (Paris: OECD, 1979).
7. *Science* 195, no. 4283 (Mar. 18, 1977).
8. Ibid., pp. 1085.
9. *North-South: A Programme for Survival* (London: Pan Books, 1980), Ch. 11.
10. OECD, *Economic Outlook* no. 19 (July 1976): Table 11.
11. OECD, *Interfutures* (Paris: OECD 1979), pp. 89, 92, 409.

5

THE GLOBAL PERSPECTIVE

GROWING INTERDEPENDENCE

There are three reasons why it is essential to see the present inflation-unemployment syndrome of modern societies in a global perspective:

1. There is a growing interdependence of all national economies.
2. The West is a diminishing part of the world economy. It must, therefore, adjust itself to changing relations with the East and the South.
3. Many non-Western countries have inflation and unemployment problems. Sometimes these are much more serious than those of the West; and though the nature of the problems is often rather different from that of the Western problems, there are also points of resemblance. I therefore think that some of the considerations of this study will be relevant in non-Western countries as well as in the West.

The main part of this chapter will be devoted to the relations of the West with the East and the South mentioned under point 2 above. By way of introduction, some remarks will be made about the more general problems referred to under point 1. Countries are becoming more and more interdependent for various reasons, all of which have to do with the continued advance of science and technology.

Trade between countries is growing faster than production. During 1963-73 the world commodity output grew by 6 percent per year, but world exports rose by 8.5 percent per year.[1] In the following difficult period, 1973-78, growth was slower, and exports of minerals actually declined by 0.5 percent per year; but for agricultural products, exports grew by 4 percent per year, compared with only 2.5 percent for production. And for manufactures, the growth rates were 5.5 and 4 percent, respectively.

It is therefore, on the average, an increasing part of the goods produced that is traded between countries. As a consequence the terms of trade are an important factor in each national economy. Are export prices rising compared with import prices, or is it the other way round? Furthermore, as discussed earlier, both inflation and unemployment can be transmitted from one country to another through international trade.

International direct investment has been growing even faster than international trade. Through most of the postwar period, it has been rising at twice the rate of world GNP.[2] This investment is undertaken by the multinational corporations, which have become a really important factor in the world economy. According to the Brandt Report quoted earlier in this study, they control between a quarter and a third of all world production, and the total sales of their foreign affiliates in 1976 were estimated at $830 billion.[3] This compares with the $991 billion world exports in the same year. And the "intra-firm trade" of the multinationals has been estimated to be more than 30 percent of all world trade.

The transfer pricing of the multinationals was referred to in Chapter 3 as part of the inflation problem. It is equally important that the multinationals are transferring Western technology to the other parts of the world on a large scale, and training workers and technicians in less-developed countries. The decision making of multinationals can influence the national economies concerned in various ways. Usually they must have the permission of the government to invest in a certain country, but they can produce more or less there, and as a rule nothing prevents them from closing down if they so desire. It is worth noting that in these ways they can influence the economies of their home countries just as well as those of the host countries in which they are working. What they are doing on a large scale is transferring production from high-wage countries in the West to low-wage countries in the South.

Another factor that is making countries dependent on events outside their borders is the growing importance of international capital movements. Because private banking is becoming internationalized, financial capital now moves easily from one country to another. Countries can to some extent defend themselves against capital movements that are considered undesirable, but their possibilities in this respect are not unlimited. And sometimes they have to choose between two possible decisions, neither of which is desirable.

If, to give an example, large amounts of U.S. dollars are offered for sale in Switzerland, the Swiss National Bank may be faced with such a difficult choice. It can buy the dollars with Swiss francs. In that case the money stock in Switzerland will increase, which may have inflationary effects. Or it may refuse to buy the dollars, the result being a fall in the value of the dollar compared with the Swiss franc. This will reduce the international competitiveness of industry in Switzerland, and thereby bring about some unemployment.

In these various ways each national economy can be influenced by the policies pursued in other countries, and also by private transactions and the outcome of wage negotiations on which it has no influence. This growing interdependence of countries and regions has intensified the need for the capacity of the economic systems to adjust themselves to changes coming from the outside. What is new is that this interdependence has now been extended to the world economy, to an extent that was unthinkable a few decades ago.

GLOBAL DEVELOPMENT

The development process is such that all national economies are developing because of the continued advance of science and technology. I have described the process more specifically in a previous book.[4] Here a few indications may suffice.

More and more, technical and other knowledge is applied to the two original factors of production, land and labor, in order to increase their productivity. To apply more knowledge, capital has to be invested—for example, in cattle, machinery, ships, railroads, buildings, or scientific equipment. Knowledge and capital are, therefore, two additional factors of production, and they are the true factors of development. Knowledge can increase the productivity of labor through education and training.

The development process thus consists of adding more and more knowledge and capital to land and labor. In this respect some countries are more advanced than others, and as a whole the modern societies of the West are economically the most highly developed. It is, however, in the nature of knowledge that it tends to spread, and therefore the less-developed countries have the possibility of gradually catching up with the more developed ones.

In order to study this process, in my previous book I divided the world's countries with more than 1 million inhabitants into seven groups, according to their income levels (GNP per capita). A country can have a high income level solely because it is particularly rich in natural resources, but as a general rule the income level is a fairly good indicator of the degree of economic development.

In Table 5.1 the countries are grouped in this way, according to

TABLE 5.1: Economic Growth, 1960-70 and 1970-77 (percent per year)

Group	GNP per Capita, 1967 (U.S. dollars)	1960-70			1970-77		
		Population	GNP	GNP per Capita	Population	GNP	GNP per Capita
1	1,801-	1.2	4.6	3.4	0.7	2.9	2.2
2	1,101-1,800	0.8	4.3	3.5	0.8	4.0	3.2
3	701-1,100	1.2	7.8	6.5	1.0	5.5	4.5
4	401-700	2.2	6.7	4.4	2.1	5.8	3.6
5	201-400	2.9	5.9	2.9	2.7	7.4	4.6
6	101-200	2.5	5.2	2.6	1.9	6.3	4.3
7	-100	2.2	3.9	1.7	2.2	3.9	1.7
	Total	2.0	5.3	3.2	1.8	4.2	2.4

Source: World Bank Atlas, 1969, 1972, 1979 (Washington: World Bank, 1969, 1972, 1980), pp. 2-3, 2-3, 6 & 8 respectively.

their income levels in 1967 for the period 1960-70 and in 1974 for the period 1970-77. For the latter period the income indicators are 2.5 times those for the first period. This corresponds approximately to the average income increase between the two years, which reflects inflation more than real growth.

It will be seen that the highest growth rates are achieved by the groups in the middle of the table. They are catching up with the rich countries in the first two groups. This was to be expected, because when countries have reached a certain stage in the development process, they can begin to take over the advanced techniques that the rich countries already have. This is how the West is transferring technology to the other regions, and how middle-income countries are gaining strength.

At the lower end of the table are the very poor countries. They are making slow progress because their educational, and often their nutritional, standards are so low that the people can do only simple work. Techniques that require more skill and more effort are suited for only a small minority of their populations.

However, even slow progress lays some of the foundations for further progress, and therefore some of the really poor countries will gradually begin to achieve somewhat higher growth rates. Eventually this may happen to most of them, but high prices of energy and increasing pressure on the land will probably result in a fairly long waiting time for some of the tropical countries, for reasons to be discussed below.

Since middle-income countries have the strong position indicated above, one gets a clearer picture by grouping the countries in three main categories, as is done in Table 5.2.

I have found it correct to list Group 6 among the low-income countries (LICsb0 for the first period but among middle-income countries (MICs) for the second, because its growth rate of GNP per capita increased substantially between the two periods. High-income countries (HICs) are represented by Groups 1 and 2 in both periods. (It should be remembered that a certain country can be in a different group in each period. Thus, Japan moved from Group 3 to Group 2 and China from Group 7 to Group 6. The main oil-exporting countries also moved upward.)

The main conclusion to be drawn from this table is that the MICs are becoming an increasingly important factor in the world economy. Including China, they have more than half of the world's population and their total GNP is growing nearly twice as fast as that of the HICs.

Where the gap is growing is between the MICs and the LICs.

TABLE 5.2: Economic Growth; Three Categories of Countries, 1960-70 and 1970-77

	1960-70				
			Annual Growth		
	Population, 1967 (million)	*GNP, 1967 (billion dollars)*	*Population*	*GNP*	*GNP per Capita*
HICs	539.6	1,303.3	1.0	4.5	3.5
MICs	904.0	583.1	1.9	7.4	5.4
LICs	1,947.6	188.1	2.3	4.3	2.0
Total	3,391.2	2,074.5	2.0	5.3	3.2
	1970-77				
			Annual Growth		
	Population, 1974 (million)	*GNP, 1974 (billion dollars)*	*Population*	*GNP*	*GNP per Capita*
HICs	690.2	3,618.3	0.7	3.2	2.5
MICs	2,018.3	1,816.9	1.9	6.0	4.0
LICs	1,105.0	154.7	2.2	3.9	1.7
Total	3,813.5	5,589.9	1.8	4.2	2.4

Source: World Bank Atlas, 1972, 1979 (Washington: World Bank, 1972, 1980), pp. 2-3, 6 & 8 **respectively.**

Nearly all the countries left in the latter group are situated in the tropical zone, and in countries like India and Bangladesh the population density will reach high levels during the next century before the world's total population stabilizes. The special problems due to the tropical climate belong to the field of science and technology, in which much remains to be done.

WEST, EAST, AND SOUTH

In Table 5.1 Groups 1 and 2 are dominated by countries of the West, while Group 3 is dominated by countries of the East and the remaining groups by countries of the South. This illustrates the historically important fact that the West has been leading in the technical and economic development that has created the present world economy. The expansion of the other parts of the world is, to a considerable extent, due to influences emanating from the West. Western medicine has helped to reduce death rates and thereby has sparked a population growth that may continue for another century before it fades. And Western science and technology have spread over the world, and thereby contributed more than anything else to productivity growth in the two other parts of the international community.

The roles are changing, however, and increasingly so. One gets a clearer picture of this by grouping the countries covered by Tables 5.1 and 5.2 according to the three-group model that I have found it useful to apply to some parts of this study. This is done in Table 5.3.

This table shows clearly that the West is now a declining part of the world economy. The two other parts are growing faster, and the differences have been considerable since 1970. For the South this is

TABLE 5.3: The West, the East, and the South: 1960-70 and 1970-77

	1960-70				
	Population, 1964 (million)	GNP, 1967 (billion dollars)	Annual Growth: Population	Annual Growth: GNP	Annual Growth: GNP per Capita
West	693.9	1,409.0	1.1	5.1	4.0
East	336.6	320.2	1.1	6.6	5.4
South	2,360.7	345.3	2.4	5.0	2.5
Total	3,391.2	2,074.5	2.0	5.3	3.2
	1970-77				
	Population, 1974 (million)	GNP, 1974 (billion dollars)	Annual Growth: Population	Annual Growth: GNP	Annual Growth: GNP per Capita
West	740.2	3,614.9	0.8	3.2	2.4
East	357.6	816.3	0.8	5.6	4.8
South	2,715.7	1,113.7	2.2	6.4	4.1
Total	3,813.5	5,544.9	1.8	4.2	2.4

Source: World Bank Atlas, 1972, 1979 (Washington: World Bank, 1972, 1980), pp. 2-3, 6 & 8 respectively.

due partly to the oil price rises but, as will be shown below, the main reason is that the continued development process is allowing more and more countries to begin to catch up with the technically more advanced societies.

For the same reason the East is catching up with the West. The USSR and the countries of Eastern Europe are less developed than the main parts of the Western world. Therefore, they can make progress by taking over techniques that have been developed in the West.

It is interesting to note that the weakening of the economic performance of the West in the 1970s has not been accompanied by a corresponding weakening in the other two regions. The industrial countries of the West are particularly sensitive to higher energy prices because of their large energy consumption. And, of course, the continued development process must bring many MICs closer to the standards of the HICs.

Earlier in this book it was discussed how inflation and unemployment can be transmitted from one country to another. Development also can be transmitted between countries, and this has happened throughout the ages. In ancient Greece vases and other earthenware products were exported to the colonies in Asia Minor during a certain period, but later the production of these goods was increasingly transferred to the colonies.

It is not surprising that this transmission of development has gathered momentum in the postwar period. Nearly all parts of the world are sovereign states, and it has been a natural goal for the governments of new countries to further the development of their economies. At the same time, the unusual progress that has taken place in transport and communication has facilitated the transfer to technology and production between countries. The importance of distance has been reduced drastically.

Fundamentally, development is an internal process in the societies concerned. What can be transmitted between countries are impulses and means of production that have to be absorbed in ways acceptable to the recipient country. Often this represents an encounter between very different cultures, and people from the West who have been engaged in this process have had to adapt themselves to tasks that are very different from those they have had at home.

But, in addition, the Western economies as a whole must be adjusted to the changing patterns of trade and production. It is general experience that the more countries industrialize, the more they export industrial goods to one another. Therefore, the continuing industrialization of the East and the South means that Western industries will be exposed to increased competition both in the markets of the other two parts of the world and in the West itself. At the same time there will be expanding markets for the more sophisticated products of Western industry in the other two parts of the world.

Two aspects of these changing patterns deserve to be mentioned. One is that the role of multinational corporations will become even more important than it is today. The other is that both the East and the South are increasingly competing with the West in the international capital markets, where both of them must attract capital for their development.

EAST-WEST RELATIONS

The adjustments that will be needed in the West, because of changing relations with the East, are different from those resulting from changes in the relations with the South. This has to do with the special nature of the politico-economic systems of the East. In principle these are of the same character in the USSR and in the East European countries. In practice there are, however, some differences between the ways in which the systems are allowed to work.

There has also been a remarkable difference between the economic performance of the USSR and that of Eastern Europe in the 1970s, and it seems likely that this has to do with the different ways in which the systems are operated. It also has some influence on the problems of adjustment with which the Western economies are faced because of their relations with the East. It is therefore worthwhile to examine the changes that have taken place.

In the first part of the postwar period, the East was, generally speaking, in what has been called the extensive phase of industrialization. Relatively simple types of industry were built up, and there was an ample supply of labor because people moved out of agriculture on a fairly large scale.

This relatively easy process has been terminated in most of the countries concerned. Increasingly they have come into what has been called the intensive phase of industrialization. The industries that have been established in recent years are at higher technological levels, and at the same time the migration out of agriculture has slowed, so that the supply of labor is not growing as fast as earlier. As a consequence an effort has been made to establish industries with techniques that are sophisticated, labor-saving, and capital-intensive.

This transition seems to have succeeded well in Eastern Europe, while the results have been disappointing in the USSR, as can be seen from Table 5.4.

The difference between the performance of Eastern Europe and of the USSR is remarkable. Economic growth has been speeding up in Eastern Europe but slowing down in the USSR. This has happened even though Eastern Europe must have been affected more than the USSR by the slowdown in the West, while the rising energy prices should be favorable to the USSR.

It is, therefore, worth noting that the East European countries have liberalized their economic systems much more since the 1960s than has the USSR. They have decentralized decision making and allowed their state enterprises not only to make dispositions more similar than before to those being made in market economies, but also to deal more with the West. Trade between Eastern Europe and the West has expanded considerably, and Western enterprises have been engaged in investment in Eastern Europe and in industrial cooperation with its enterprises. The USSR has been much more cautious in these various fields.

This points to the conclusion that more efficient working methods have contributed to the relatively successful performance of the East European economies in the 1970s. Since these procedures have also intensified economic relations between the East and the West, it is a question of great importance whether a similar liberalization can be expected in the USSR in the years to come. If that happens, East-West relations may become a more important factor than it is today.

Some aspects of development in the East can influence the

TABLE 5.4: Economic Growth in the East, 1960-70 and 1970-77, (percent per year)

	1960-70			*1970-77*		
	Population	*GNP*	*GNP per Capita*	*Population*	*GNP*	*GNP per Capita*
Eastern Europe	0.7	5.8	5.1	0.5	6.3	5.6
USSR	1.3	7.0	5.6	0.9	5.3	4.4
Total	1.1	6.6	5.4	0.8	5.6	4.8

Source: World Bank Atlas, 1972, 1979 (Washington: World Bank, 1972, 1980), pp. 2-3, 6&8 respectively.

employment situation in the West. In recent years the East has had a balance-of-payments deficit that has resulted in a growing debt. It has been estimated that this group of countries will be a net importer of capital for a number of years to come, and this may be a natural consequence of the transition to a period with more capital-intensive methods of production. The East will, therefore, compete with the West in the international capital markets, where it has already been a borrower for some years.

In order to limit their deficits, the Eastern countries have sometimes used restrictive methods of trade that can have a disturbing effect on other countries. This has happened in a period when trade in general has been difficult, both for the West and for most parts of the South.

There are three methods that Eastern countries have used to different degrees and that have to do with the special character of their economic systems. First, they can reduce their imports at fairly short notice to improve their balance-of-payments situation. Those who depend on exports to the East must, therefore, be prepared for changes that can have a negative influence on employment. Second, in order to increase exports, Eastern countries can offer goods or services for sale at prices that are too low for Western enterprises to meet.

Third, as a condition of placing orders with Western enterprises, Eastern countries can request that these Western firms buy Eastern products for which they have no use. They must, therefore, try to sell them in the Western markets. This last procedure has played an important role in recent years. Because of the generally weak situation in large parts of the world markets, Western firms cannot easily refuse to place such orders. The result may, however, be that other Western firms are exposed to additional competition because the Eastern products may have to be sold at low prices in order to be sold at all.

These three methods have in common the fact that disturbances, which are often unpredictable, can have a negative influence on employment. Since it is one of the problems of modern Western societies at the present stage of their development that their methods of adjustment to change are not flexible enough, this should be taken into account.

An intensification of East-West economic relations is desirable from many points of view, and there are considerable possibilities, especially if the practices of the USSR should become more flexible, like those of Eastern Europe. But this will also increase the need for flexibility in the Western economic systems.

SOUTH-WEST RELATIONS

It can be seen from Table 5.3 that during the 1970s the South has been a factor of growing importance in the world economy. Its total GNP grew twice as fast as that of the West from 1970 to 1977. This is, of course, partly due to the oil price rises since 1973. All the major oil-exporting countries belong to the South. At the same time these price rises have, however, had a negative influence on the economies of the majority of Southern countries that are oil importers.

The development of the South is, therefore, a more complicated process. Since the modern societies of the West will be influenced more and more by this development, especially as regards employment, a closer look at this process must be part of the present study. In Table 5.5 the countries of the South have been divided in four subgroups in order to give a more complete picture than the one in Table 5.3.

The member countries of OPEC are obviously a group of particular interest because of their very large revenues from oil exports after 1973.

The newly industrializing countries (NICs) are a group of MICs that have become exporters of manufactures on an increasing scale. They are, therefore, of special interest as competitors to the industries of the West. In Table 5.8 a list will be given of the NICs that are included as a subgroup in Table 5.5.

"Other South" consists of the countries of the South that do not belong to one of the other two groups. That the LICs of "Other South" are a much larger group in the first period than in the second is due mainly to the fact that China had moved upward and become an MIC before 1974. As a consequence the MICs are a larger group in the second period than in the first.

Table 5.5 shows some remarkable differences among the subgroups, especially for the second period. Both the OPEC member countries and the NICs have much higher growth rates than the countries of the West. Most of the OPEC countries and all the NICs now belong to the broad category of MICs. It also is interesting to note that the other parts of the South that are MICs are growing substantially faster than the industrial countries.

It has sometimes been asserted that the economic growth of the South depends greatly on the degree of prosperity in the West, since the industrial countries are the main markets for the exports of the poorer nations. This dependency on Western markets, however, seems to be of declining importance. Table 5.5 shows higher growth rates for the MICs in the 1970s than in the 1960s; there was a clear change in the opposite direction in the West.

TABLE 5.5: Development of the South, 1960-70 and 1970-77

	1960-70				
			Annual Growth		
	Population, 1964 million)	*GNP 1967, (billion dollars)*	*Population*	*GNP*	*GNP per Capita*
OPEC	216.1	34.1	2.6	4.8	2.1
NICs	224.2	48.7	3.0	6.2	3.1
Other South					
MICs	243.4	105.3	2.4	5.7	3.2
LICs	1,677.0	157.2	2.3	4.2	1.9
Total	2,360.7	345.3	2.4	5.0	2.5
	1970-77				
			Annual Growth		
	Population, 1974 (million)	*GNP 1974, (billion dollars)*	*Population*	*GNP*	*GNP per Capita*
OPEC	256.4	124.7	2.4	8.4	5.9
NICs	268.4	178.8	2.6	9.0	6.2
Other South					
MICs	1,214.3	667.3	2.0	6.0	3.9
LICs	976.6	132.9	2.3	3.3	1.0
Total	2,715.7	1,103.7	2.2	6.4	4.1

Note: Iran is not included in OPEC because information for 1970-77 was not available.

Source: World Bank Atlas, 1972, 1979 (Washington: World Bank, 1972, 1980), pp. 2-3, 6 & 8 respectively

In actual fact, the development of the South has been less and less dependent on the situation in the West for a fairly long time. According to World Bank statistics, the annual growth in percent of GNP in the West and the South has been as shown below.[5]

	1961-65	*1966-73*	*1974-78*
Industrialized countries	5.6	4.9	2.4
Developing countries	5.9	6.6	5.4

It will be seen that during 1966-73, when economic growth was slowing down in the West, this did not prevent the South from speeding up its growth rates.

It is, therefore, important to stress that the development process continues even in years when the export conditions are not as good as before. This is particularly true as regards the MICs where the standards of education and training have reached such levels that more and more advanced techniques can be introduced.

Table 5.5 does, however, show a much weaker performance in the LICs. A comparison between the two periods covered by the table can be misleading in this case because China was an LIC in 1967 but an MIC in 1974. I have, therefore, calculated the annual growth rate of GNP per capita in 1960-70 for exactly the same group of countries that were listed as LICs in 1974. This growth rate was 1.3 percent. For this group of really poor countries the years 1970-77 therefore showed a deterioration in their growth performance.

It is not likely, however, that this has much to do with development in the West. Nearly all the LICs covered by the table are situated in South Asia and tropical Africa; agriculture is still a dominant activity there, and they are exposed to the vagaries of the tropical climate, especially the monsoon in the Indian subcontinent. Much, therefore, depends on the output of agriculture and its fluctuations, which can be very considerable. The World Bank annual reports for 1978 and 1979 contain the following information about the growth rates for agricultural production and GNP in 1973-77.[6]

	South Asia		*Tropical Africa*	
	Agriculture	*GNP*	*Agriculture*	*GNP*
1973	8.4	4.4	-3.0	4.9
1974	-4.5	1.4	7.4	8.1
1975	9.9	8.4	1.1	1.0
1976	-1.7	2.5	2.5	6.2
1977	7.6	5.8	0.5	4.4

For South Asia in particular there is a close correlation between the fluctuations in agriculture and in the economy as a whole.

It is a matter of concern in the world community that the performance of the LICs is so much poorer than that of the other countries. A few further indications will show that this has more to do with the main subject of this book than one would suppose at first sight.

The fact that the tropical South is still so dependent on agriculture has a wider perspective. Not only are there troublesome fluctuations in the harvest, but the tropical climate is marked by diseases of plants, animals, and human beings, and too little is known about how to make tropical agriculture more rational. To this is added a growing shortage of land, which will force people to move out of agriculture to an extent that can have far-reaching consequences for the international development of the labor markets and, thus, for the employment situation.

I have, therefore, shown in Table 5.6 the relations between the population and the land available in the same categories of countries as those covered by Table 5.2 for 1960-70. Two conclusions can be drawn from this table:

1. The LICs (and here this includes China) are short of land in relation to their total population, and this shortage will become more pronounced in the decades to come because of their rapid population growth. The possibility of turning permanent grass into arable land is poorer than in the two richer categories of countries.
2. The shortage of land is even more severe in relation to their agricultural population, which is still very large. This is why the migration of people out of agriculture can be expected to continue on a large scale for many years to come.

The major part of this manpower will be available for industry. A rapidly growing labor force will, therefore, counteract any tendency for wages to rise. Since the quality of the labor force will be rising, because of the progress taking place in education and training, wages will probably be kept fairly low, compared with the quality of labor, for a long time.

Those employed in the West will have to compete with this growing, cheap labor force of the South. Therefore, the problem of adjusting to the changing influences from other parts of the world will probably be more serious than is generally being recognized.

In this respect it should be remembered that unemployment is not a problem only in the West. There is already some unemployment in various parts of the South, and in addition there is much underemployment, part of which may be turned into open unemployment in the years to come.

This underemployment is difficult to estimate. There is, of course, much underemployment in agriculture, where the work to be done varies throughout the year. There is, however, also fairly high underemployment in the towns and cities, because many of those who are coming in from the rural areas in the hope of finding jobs can find work only at intervals and for short periods.

The ILO has made an estimate of the unemployment and underemployment in the South. The main results are shown in Table 5.7.

TABLE 5.6: Relations Between People and Land, 1970

	Population			Ha Land, per Capita			
				of Total Population		of Population in Agriculture	
	Total (million)	In Agriculture (millions)	Percent Agriculture	Arable	Permanent Grass	Arable	Permanent Grass
HICs	556.3	43.9	7.9	.61	1.42	7.72	18.2
MICs	956.7	364.2	38.1	.56	1.33	1.46	3.50
LICs	2,186.0	1,502.6	68.7	.26	.38	.38	.55
Total	3,699.0	1,910.7	51.7	.39	.78	.78	1.52

Source: FAO.

TABLE 5.7: Unemployment and Underemployment in the South, 1975 (percentages of the whole labor force)

	Unemployment	*Underemployment*
Asia	3.9	36.4
Africa	7.1	37.4
Latin America	5.1	28.9

Source: ILO, *Tripartite World Conference on Employment, Income Distribution and Social Progress and the International Division of Labour* (Geneva: ILO, 1976), Tables ix, xi.

It can be expected that those now listed as underemployed will increasingly appear as unemployed or as employed in industry and services. As indicated above, a large movement out of agriculture can be expected, which will no doubt reduce underemployment but increase the labor force available for industry and services. This will include shipping, since an increasing part of the world's ships are registered in the South.

In addition, the rapid population growth in the South will result in a large increase in the available labor force for many years to come. The United Nations population estimates of 1978 show the following figures for the West and the South.[7]

	1980 (million)	*2000 (million)*	*Increase (million)*
West	729	809	80
South	3,309	4,956	1,647
Total	4,038	5,765	1,727

It is part of the picture that in the West the age groups that are leaving the labor force show the fastest growth, whereas in the South those entering the working population are growing fastest.

The above considerations lead to the conclusion that the South represents markets of increasing importance and that a unique growth of the available labor force will take place in the South in the foreseeable future. This being so, it can be expected that multinational corporations will remove an increasing part of their activities to the South. Protection of industry in many countries of the South should encourage them to produce in these countries instead of exporting manufactured articles to them from plants in the West.

There have also been growing possibilities of exporting some kinds of manufactures from the West to the South. Machinery and equipment are needed, and much of these goods must be imported from the West, because the labor force of the South is not yet qualified for the more sophisticated kinds of production represented by such articles.

A new division of labor is, therefore, on the way. For some time to come, this will particularly influence the employment patterns of the West and of the so-called NICs. Some remarks about the interrelationship between these two groups of countries will be made in the next section.

NEW COMPETITORS

In recent years the world's attention has been attracted to an increasing degree by MICs that have experienced a particularly rapid economic growth. This has, as a rule, been due to a process of industrialization of such dimensions that they are becoming obvious competitors of Western industry. They have, therefore, been described in some publications as newly industrializing countries (NICs).

It is a matter of judgment which countries should be considered as belonging to this category. In Table 5.5 I included 12 countries in the subgroup NICs. Table 5.8 contains more detailed information about these countries.

All of these countries have had an overall annual growth of at least 7 percent. All of them, with the exception of Syria, also have had a rapid growth of their exports of manufactures. I have included Syria and Jordan because they have had remarkably high growth rates in spite of their war with Israel. Also, their population growth rates are very high, probably due to an influx of Palestinians, and they can count on support from oil-exporting Islamic countries. Other countries with lower growth rates, but with increasing exports of manufactures, are Mexico, Israel, and the Philippines.

What particularly strengthens the competitiveness of these countries is the fact that their prices of ordinary labor are much lower than those in the West. At the same time, the productivity of labor is approaching Western levels in some branches where the competition from NICs has been important. Table 5.9. is an extract from Table 3.5 in a recent study of the role of multinationals.[8]

Some comments on the question of labor productivity in countries at various levels of development are in order. The following sentences should be relevant in regard to the countries covered by the table:

TABLE 5.8: Newly Industrializing Countries

	Annual Growth, 1970-77 (percent)			Manufactures as Percent of Exports	
	Population	*GNP*	*GNP per Capita*	*1960*	*1976*
Singapore	1.6	8.3	6.6	26	46
Hong Kong	2.0	7.9	5.8	80	97
Brazil	2.9	9.8	6.7	3	25
Taiwan	2.0	7.6	5.5	14	85
Malaysia	2.7	7.7	4.9	6	16
Dom. Republic	3.0	7.7	4.6	2	17
Tunisia	2.0	8.6	6.5	10	26
Syria	3.3	9.6	6.1	19	10
South Korea	2.0	9.8	7.6	14	88
Jordan	3.3	10.0	6.5	4	21
Thailand	2.8	7.0	4.1	2	19
Egypt	2.1	7.4	5.2	12	27
	2.6	9.0	6.2		

Sources: World Bank Atlas, 1979 (Washington: World Bank, 1980), pp. 6 & 8. World Bank, *World Development Report.* (Washington, D.C.: World Bank, 1978), Table 7, and (1979), Table 9.

TABLE 5.9: Hourly Earnings in Assembly Plants in South and United States

	Ratio US/Country Mentioned
Electronics	
Hong Kong	11.8
Mexico	4.4
Taiwan	18.2
Machine assembly	
Hong Kong	9.7
Mexico	6.2
South Korea	10.1
Singapore	11.6
Taiwan	9.8
Semiconductors	
Hong Kong	10.3
Mexico	4.2
South Korea	10.2
Singapore	11.6
Clothing	
Mexico	4.3

Source: World Bank Atlas, 1979 (Washington: World Bank, 1980), pp. 6 & 8. World Bank, *World Development Report*, (Washington, D.C.: World Bank, 1978), Table 7, and (1979), Table 9.

> Thus, for example, the US Tariff Commission found that for electronic assembly, foreign labour productivity was about 92% of the US level, and for certain other items the productivity differential was still smaller, even negative in some cases. The greatest difference was in the case of garment making in Mexico where the labour productivity was only around 60% of the US level. . . . In more general terms, the US Tariff Commission has found that the productivity of workers in foreign establishments assembling or processing products of US origin generally approximates that of workers of the same classifications in the U.S.A.[9]

These are examples of ordinary labor in NICs that is very cheap compared with labor in the West, if quality differentials are taken into account. It can, therefore, be expected that NICs will represent an increasing proportion of world production in a number of branches where Western industry has been dominant.

What has been said about the countries covered by Table 5.8 will, in the years to come, also be true of other countries of the South as they reach similar stages in the development process. Countries representing a fairly wide range of income levels can achieve the conditions for rapid industrial development. Those covered by the table have been listed according to their GNP per capita in 1974, which varied from U.S. $2,240 in Singapore to $280 in Egypt.

In this respect it is worth noting that, as mentioned earlier, some of the LICs are poorly provided with agricultural land compared with their growing population. This is true of China and of the large LICs of South Asia: India, Pakistan, and Bangladesh. It can, therefore, be expected that they will industrialize fairly rapidly by moving an increasing part of their labor force into industry. It has been announced that this is the intention of the Chinese government, and as far as the three South Asian countries are concerned, manufactures as percentages of their exports are shown below.[10]

	1960	*1976*
India	45	53
Pakistan	27	57
Bangladesh	—	61

(Bangladesh, of course became independent only in 1971.)

It should be remembered that labor in these countries is even cheaper than in the NICs mentioned above. Competition with cheap labor in the South is, however, only part of the picture. In order to industrialize, the new competitors are importing sophisticated production equipment from the West. Some of them have, in fact, increased their imports of manufactures from the West more than their exports to the West. At the same time, they have also increased their exports of manufactures to other parts of the South, in competition with Western industries.

The total impact on employment in the West is difficult to estimate. In general the expansion in the South has been in relatively labor-intensive branches of industry, while the growth in the South's imports from the West has been in more capital-intensive branches. And the jobs taken over by the South are, on the whole, of a relatively simple nature, while the jobs created by their imports of machinery usually require more competence.

This process will, therefore, make continuous adjustments necessary in the labor markets of the West for many years to come. Gradually some of the NICs will also become competitive in more sophisticated branches. South Korea and Brazil have already made progress in shipbuilding, but the more sophisticated parts of that industry will be concentrated in the West for some years to come.

It remains to be added that while the South is rich in labor, it is still poor in capital. It will, therefore, be a net importer of capital in the foreseeable future. In this respect a few oil-exporting countries will be an exception. The countries of the Arabian Peninsula and Libya are likely to have a large balance-of-payments surplus for many years to come. It follows that the rest of the world will have a corresponding deficit.

The West must, therefore, compete for capital with both the East and the South. There will be pressure in some of the international organizations for more development aid from the rich countries. And some of the NICs have become borrowers in the commercial markets on a fairly large scale.

LABOR AND CAPITAL IN THE WORLD ECONOMY

The preceding parts of this chapter lead to the conclusion that there will be an ample supply of labor in the foreseeable future. In the West the labor supply is expected to grow slightly faster in 1975-90 than in 1960-75. The annual percentage growth rates are estimated as follows:[11]

Years	*Rate*
1960-75	1.0
1975-90	1.2

That the growth rate can be rising in spite of falling overall population growth rates is due particularly to increasing female participation in the labor force and to a reduction of the emigration from Southern Europe and Ireland.

The unemployment in 12 OECD member countries representing the main part of the West has been estimated at 5.1 percent in 1979.[12] If this figure is to be reduced to 2 percent in 1990, total employment must grow by about 1.5 percent per year. At the same time the available labor force in the South will grow several times as fast because of rapid population growth and because of the unemployment and underemployment described in Table 5.7.

This means that if labor is not to be wasted on a large scale, total employment in the world economy will have to grow much faster in the years to come than during the 1960s and 1970s.

What will be the supply of capital to be combined with these increasing quantities of labor? In the United States there has been a discussion about an approaching capital shortage for a number of years. But it is not easy to determine what should be understood by the term "capital shortage."

The supply of labor can be determined with a reasonable degree of precision. There is a certain number of persons available. The supply of capital is a more complicated concept. The existing stock of real capital has a value that depends on the future production in which it can be used. All evaluations are, therefore, uncertain. The same is true of an evaluation of the annual depreciation, the loss of value due to the fact that the various machines and other items of which the stock consists gradually wear out or become obsolete.

What is more certain is the annual addition made to the capital stock through investment. Such investment requires that total production be greater than total consumption—that is, that part of the income created by production is saved. For the world economy as a whole, the investment of a certain period is, therefore, equal to the savings of the same period. But while some countries can have a surplus of savings over investment, so that they can export capital, others will have a surplus of investment over savings, so that they must import capital. The typical situation in the foreseeable future will be that a small group of oil-exporting countries will have a large capital surplus, whereas most other countries will have deficits.

One can talk about gross investment—the total amount of new investment—or net investment—where depreciation is deducted—and, correspondingly, about gross or net savings. Usually gross figures are used because the value of depreciation is uncertain and because the quantity of new investment determines how great the possibilities are of obtaining innovations by introducing new types of machinery and equipment.

The level of gross investment is, therefore, probably the factor that, more than anything else, determines how much the production per worker can increase. If labor productivity is to increase fast, much investment will be needed. If we have to accept less advance in labor productivity, lower rates of gross investment will suffice.

The question of capital supply is, therefore, closely linked to two other questions: How much will employment increase? How much do we expect labor productivity to increase? As mentioned above, the labor force of the OECD area grew by 1.0 percent per year from 1960 to 1975. For the period of rapid economic growth from 1959-60 to 1972-73, total GNP of the same area rose by 5.5 percent per year.[13] As mentioned in Chapter 1, unemployment decreased until 1966, then increased to some extent. We can, therefore, assume that employment has grown in roughly the same proportion as the available labor force.

If this is so, labor productivity must have grown by approximately 4.5 percent per year, because 1.010 x 1.045 = 1.055. Other information seems to indicate that this is not far from the truth. As mentioned above, if unemployment in the West is to be reduced to 2 percent by 1990, employment will have to increase by about 1.5 percent per year during the period 1979-90. If labor productivity is to grow by the same percentage as during the years from 1959-60 to 1972-73, total GNP is, therefore, to grow by 6.1 percent per year (1.015 x 1.045 = 1.061).

This would mean that economic growth would have to be even faster than in the period of rapid growth, 1960-73. Rates of investment would, therefore, have to be higher than in that period—considerably higher.

That is obviously impossible. It has already been demonstrated that rapid growth in the period mentioned exposed the economies of the West to increasing pressure. Rates of inflation were increasing, as were pollution and energy consumption, and there was a gradual breakdown of the international monetary system. To this must be added that energy prices are now much higher. Energy consumption, therefore, has to be restrained and part of the investment that is possible must be devoted to oil drilling and other types of energy production.

The difficulties are increased by the fact that most Western countries will have a balance-of-payments deficit for a fairly long time to come. Countries with such deficits will normally have to pursue cautious demand management policies. The high rates of inflation we have had in recent years also call for cautious policies.

This being so, the possibilities of economic growth during the next few decades must be estimated as being much more modest than for the period 1960-73. In a report from OECD, the economic activity for the period through the year 2000 is projected as growing by 3.4 percent per year, but the rate may be about 3.5 percent to 1990.[14]

If, under such circumstances, the unemployment rate is to come down to 2 percent by 1990, the annual increase of labor productivity would be growing by only 2.0 percent per year (1.035 x 1.015 = 1.020). This would be a drastic reduction from the rate of about 4.5 percent per year for the period 1960-73. It would mean that the rates of investment could be substantially lower than in the past because methods of production would be more labor-intensive and less capital-intensive. Such a change in the capital needs of the West would correspond well to the prospects of the world capital market if there is to be a harmonious global development.

It has already been indicated that the East can be expected import capital to a significant extent for a number of years to come. The countries of the East are now in the intensive phase of industrialization described in the section "East-West Relations." They will, therefore, have more capital-intensive methods of production.

It is, however, the South in particular that can be expected to become a capital importer in the years to come. As mentioned in the previous section, the NICs are now showing high rates of economic growth, which also means high rates of investment. This will, to some extent, be financed by commercial borrowing in the international capital markets.

Other MICs have fairly high rates of economic growth and, therefore, considerable needs for capital imports. This group now includes China, which has become a member of the World Bank and thus will have access to the resources available through the World Bank system.

The LICs will be in a difficult situation, and it can be expected that in the international organizations there will be pressure on Western countries to increase their aid programs in favor of the poorest nations.

In a more general way it must be foreseen that capital will increasingly be attracted by the large, rapidly growing, cheap labor supply of the South and by the mineral resources that have not yet been discovered or have been only partly explored.

With a further development of the international capital markets, there should be a tendency toward an equalization of the the real rates of interest. This being so, capital should tend to flow more and more toward the parts of the world where it can be combined with labor that is cheap in relation to its quality. Both the banking systems and the multinational corporations can be expected to work in that direction, and this must be considered a natural consequence of the fact that the development process seems to gather momentum in large parts of the world.

From a global point of view, it is desirable that capital investment should be more equally distributed between rich and poor countries than it has been in the past. This does, however, raise serious problems for the West. The indications given above concerning labor force and labor productivity in the West can be summarized in the following percentages for the annual growth of three strategic factors in two periods:

1960-73	*Percent*
Employment	1.0
Labor productivity	4.5
GNP	5.5
1979-90	
Employment	1.5
Labor productivity	2.0

It is a modest suggestion that unemployment should be reduced from 5.1 per cent in 1979 to 2 percent in 1990. But it can, according to OECD estimates, happen only if employment is growing faster than in the period 1960-73 while the growth rates of labor productivity are reduced in a remarkable way. This is what would happen if the trends in the methods of production were changed so that more people were employed for each percent of production growth.

We have gone through a long period when the methods of production have become more and more capital-intensive. We can reach a much better employment situation in 1990 if this trend is replaced by one that requires more labor and less capital than would a continued development along the traditional lines. Methods would then be more labor-intensive than they will be if the systems continue to work as they do today.

The trouble is that the limited quantities of investment that have been made during the last few years are still of the very capital-intensive type because the real price of capital is still negative for a large part of of the investors, while the real price of labor is still rising in many countries.

Modern societies are, therefore, not adjusted to the changed conditions in the world economy. This is why the last chapter of this book will be devoted largely to the question of how the methods of adjustment can be improved.

NOTES

1. GATT, *International Trade 1978/79* (Geneva: GATT, 1979), Table 1.
2. Christopher Tugendhat, *The Multinationals* (Harmondsworth: Penguim Books, 1977), p. 45.
3. *North-South: A Programme for Survival* (London: Pan Books, 1980).
4. Thorkil Kristensen, *Development in Rich and Poor Countries* (New York: Praeger, 1974).
5. World Bank, *Annual Report, 1978, 1979* (Washington, D.C.: World Bank, 1978 & 1979), Statistical Annex, Table 1.
6. World Bank, *Annual Report 1978 and 1979* (Washington, D.C.: World Bank, 1978 & 1979), Statistical Annex Table 1.
7. *World Population Trends and Prospects by Country* (New York: United Nations, 1979), first Table.
8. The International Division of Labour and Multinational Companies, *Report from a Symposium* (Westmead, England: Saxon House, 1979), p. 104.
9. Ibid., p. 106.
10. World Bank, *World Development Report* (Washington, D.C.: World Bank, 1979), Annex, Table 9.
11. OECD, *Demographic Trends 1950-1990* (Paris: OECD, 1979), p. 32.
12. OECD, *Economic Outlook* no. 26 (1979): Table 13.
13. OECD, *Economic Outlook* no. 19 (1976): Table 1.
14. *Interfutures* (Paris: OECD, 1979), p. 92.

6

POLICY ISSUES

It may be useful to begin this last chapter by giving a short summary of the main conclusions to be drawn from the analysis undertaken in the preceding chapters. It is important to have a reasonably clear understanding of the nature of the present crisis before one begins to discuss what can be done to improve the working of the economic systems.

Such a summary can be constructed in various ways. In what follows, I have tried to give an outline of the nature of the difficulties that characterize the modern economies during the present phase of their development. It concentrates on six major aspects of the causal relations behind the crisis.

A GRADUAL DEVELOPMENT

The present combination of inflation and unemployment has developed over a fairly long period. There has been some inflation ever since 1945. Unemployment reached its minimum in 1966, and on the whole it increased, first slowly and later more rapidly, during the last years of the period of rapid economic growth that ended in 1973. Since then it has continued at fairly high levels.

The international monetary system, based on fixed but adjustable exchange rates, was gradually breaking down, primarily because some countries had much more inflation than others, but also because of other disturbances of the balances of payments in important countries. The linkage of the U.S. dollar with gold was restricted in 1968 and completely abolished in 1971, and since March 1973 floating exchange rates have played a dominant role, thereby enhancing inflationary tendencies in various countries.

Finally, the period of rapid economic growth in the West came to a standstill in the first half of 1973. In June of that year *The Economist* forecast the following two years' decline of production in the OECD area and came remarkably close to the truth.

The disturbances mentioned above all took place before the first great oil price rise at the end of 1973. They must, therefore, have something to do with internal weaknesses in the working of the economic systems of Western industrial societies. It should, perhaps, be added that during the Great Depression of the 1930s, unemployment reached very high levels. At that time there was, on the whole, no inflation. But if more expansionary policies had been pursued, as suggested by John Maynard Keynes, there would probably have been some inflation, combined with somewhat lower rates of unemployment. The situation would then have had some similarities with the present situation.

It was demonstrated in Chapter 1 how in earlier times self-adjusting forces were at work, and thus—while prices, wages, and employment could move up and down during the business cycles—the economies were never locked in a situation of inflation or unemployment for any length of time.

These self-adjusting forces have gradually lost more and more of their efficacy. In the 1930s there was much unemployment all the time. In the postwar period there has been inflation all the time, and gradually the two evils have been combined in such a way that they both threaten to continue year after year.

The question of how we have come to this situation will be discussed below.

THE ROLE OF ORGANIZATION

The markets of former times were largely unorganized. There were many buyers and sellers, and none of them were dominant. This is why prices and wages could move up and down as market conditions varied. Over a long period markets have, however, become more and more organized. Because of modern techniques, numerous branches of industry are now dominated by a few very large enterprises that are strong enough to determine their own prices.

Labor, too, has been organized, and though there are also employers' associations, labor unions are often in a strong position. Large parts of the business sector can pass on much of the wage rises to consumers through price rises because of their market power. And modern enterprises can lose substantial amounts during a strike or lockout because they have large fixed costs.

The organization of capital markets is more complicated. Private banks have become larger, and many of them operate in several countries and in currencies other than that of their home country. This has facilitated international capital movements. At the national level, governments and central banks have acquired increased responsibility because the monetary systems have been detached from gold. The national authorities must now decide the amount of money to circulate in the country. Internationally, the IMF, the World Bank, and other institutions have been given responsibility for the transfer of capital to countries that need it.

It should be added that in most countries a large public sector has organized education, health care, and other services. Fiscal policy has, therefore, become important. Total demand can be influenced through changes in taxation or in public expenditure. Prices in agriculture often are deliberately influenced by political decisions and, through price controls and changes of exchange rates, the system of prices can be influenced in a more general way.

Between them these changes have had the effect that the old system of self-adjusting forces has, to a large extent, been replaced by a new system of decision making at various levels. Large enterprises decide what their prices will be, especially if they have a strong market power. Wages are decided by collective bargaining between large organizations. The size of total demand depends on decisions regarding fiscal and monetary policies, and the supply of financial capital depends on decisions made by a multitude of private and public institutions at national or international levels.

The trouble is that at the present stage of the development of organization, decision making in the various institutions is to a large extent uncoordinated. The fixing of prices, wages, taxes, exchange rates, and so on is not a coherent system because the various decision makers can have different intentions.

This being so, it is not surprising that the economies are not working well. We have lost an old, largely self-adjusting system, and the new, complicated system has not yet developed coherent methods of adjustment.

THE OIL PRICE RISES

The establishment and growth of OPEC is an obvious example of the new importance of organizations. And it shows how powerful decision making can be. The limited size of the world's oil reserves and their geographical concentration was bound to give the main exporters of this convenient source of energy a unique market power. If this had been foreseen in time, prices might have been raised gradually over a longer period and there would have been more time to prepare for energy conservation and the development of alternative sources of energy.

As it is now, the oil price rises will affect the Western economies in various ways, and they will increase the need for these economies to be able to adjust to change. Thus, they also throw light on the way the economic systems function. The oil price rises reinforce inflation. Their direct effect on the national price levels is limited, but there are considerable indirect effects because the wage/price spiral will be pushed each time the oil price is raised.

Unemployment is also being reinforced. Consumption in many oil-importing countries will be influenced in a negative way; the production of automobiles has already suffered perceptibly. The fact that higher oil prices make people poorer should induce them to work more, but as the systems function, the result is less work.

Another result will be that a few oil-exporting countries will have a large balance-of-payments surplus for many years to come. The modern organization of the capital markets will facilitate the recycling of funds that this necessitates, but since many oil-importing countries will have a balance-of-payments deficit, they will feel forced to pursue cautious economic policies.

For the world economy as a whole, this means that economic growth will be slower than it otherwise would have been. The need for the economies to adjust to lower growth rates will, thus, be one of the problems discussed in this chapter.

INFLATION AND UNEMPLOYMENT

Continued high rates of inflation and unemployment are the two main economic problems of modern societies. Demand management, which was considered a powerful instrument in the first postwar years, cannot combat the present combination of these two evils effectively.

If demand is increased through expansionary policies, there will be more inflation, and unemployment may be reduced only temporarily. If demand is restricted, there will be more unemployment, and the rate of inflation is not likely to be reduced in an appreciable way. This was demonstrated in Chapter 3 and illustrated by Figure 3.1.

It should be clear from Chapters 3 and 4 that the present types of organization in modern societies tend to give rise to both inflation and unemployment. Because of market power in large parts of the business sector, prices are, on the whole, kept rising all the time. If there is a recession with falling prices of raw materials, enterprises will often be able to increase their price markups so that the prices of their products will not fall.

As regards wages, labor unions have, on the whole, been in a strong position during the postwar period. Not only have they gained more and more organizational strength; the very fact that, to a large extent, enterprises are able to determine the prices of their products makes it relatively easy for them to accept wage increases. They can, on a large scale, pass them on to consumers through higher prices. At the same time, they have high fixed costs that must be covered even if production comes to a standstill during a strike or lockout. This makes it preferable to avoid such a standstill, even if higher wages and prices have to be accepted.

Now, if higher wages lead to higher prices, wage earners will find that their real wages are not much higher than they were. The result may then be new requests for wage rises, which lead to new price rises, and so on. This is how we have gotten the wage/price spiral that has become a characteristic feature of postwar inflation. Because of the increasingly strong organization in the product and labor markets, this is fundamentally a price/cost-push inflation. If these markets had remained largely unorganized, prices and wages would have moved up and down as in former times.

It is relatively easy to understand that market organization must lead to inflation, pushing prices and wages upward all the time. But why does it also lead to unemployment? The answer to that question is, roughly speaking, that in the process described above, not all prices rise in the same proportion. Therefore, some disharmonies occur in the system of prices. There are two such disharmonies in particular that have had a negative influence on employment. They are described in Chapters 3 and 4, and they may be briefly outlined as below.

First, though some parts of the business sector have relatively strong market power, so that they can raise their prices without much loss of sales when wages rise, others are in a weaker position. They are exposed to more competition, so that the possibility of price rises is much more limited. This can be seen from Table 3.1 and is illustrated in Figures 4.1 and 4.2.

Both types of enterprises must, however, compete for labor in the same labor market. As a consequence their wages rise in roughly the same proportion, as can be seen from Table 3.1. This means that in the parts of the economy where competition is keener, wages rise so much more than prices that production becomes unprofitable in many cases.

This being so, enterprises have two possibilities for survival. They can give up the parts of their production that have become unprofitable. Or they can try to reduce their costs by introducing new methods of production that are more labor-saving and capital-intensive than the former methods.

In both cases employment will be reduced. This change in the relationship between the price of labor and the prices of some of the goods to be produced is, thus, one of the causes of the new type of continued unemployment.

Second is a change in the relationship between the price of labor and the real price of capital. It was demonstrated in Chapter 3 that because of inflation, the real rate of interest is now negative for many of the persons or enterprises who borrow in order to invest. Interest and repayment of the loans can be paid with money that is worth less and less compared with the money borrowed.

It follows that when the price of labor is positive and the real price of capital is negative, it is profitable to invest any quantity of capital if it means that labor can be saved. This is why, during recent decades, techniques have become more and more capital-intensive and labor-saving. This trend has been dominant for many years, and it has contributed substantially to the present high level of unemployment.

It can, thus, be concluded that the growing importance of market organization is the main cause of the new, persistent types of inflation and unemployment. Market organization in the product and labor markets is pushing prices and wages upward, with no opposite movements during the recessions. This process is facilitated by the new types of organization in the capital markets that make financial capital easily available.

The same process leads to unemployment because two price relationships are changed. Labor becomes too expensive, compared with product prices, in the parts of the economy where there is still relatively strong competition. And the real price of capital has become so low—often negative—that there are strong arguments for replacing labor with capital. In this case inflation is a direct cause of unemployment.

It is particularly important to notice that in these new ways of functioning of the system, the old self-adjusting forces have to a large extent disappeared. If prices and wages are pushed upward, no countervailing forces are pushing them down again, as happened during the business cycles in former times. And if unemployment is created, there are no self-adjusting forces that will move the economy back toward full employment.

Decision making plays a major role in the modern societies, but the various decisions are to a large extent uncoordinated. Inflation and unemployment will continue as long as this is so.

ADJUSTMENT TO CHANGES

We have seen that the modern economies do not have self-adjusting forces that are sufficiently effective to bring them back close to price stability and full employment. Another difficulty is that they do not easily adjust to changes that influence them from the outside. This has already been demonstrated in regard to the oil price rises of recent years. It is, however, a problem of a more general nature.

No clear distinction can be made between changes that influence the system from the outside and changes that at least partly have their roots in the system itself. This is, however, not very important. Technological changes can have their roots in a new relationship between the prices of labor and capital, or they can have them in new discoveries in science. In both cases they are perceived by the enterprises as coming from the outside, and they must find out how to react to these changes.

Similarly, the necessity of accepting lower rates of economic growth can be explained by the fact that the rapid growth in the years from 1960 to 1973 had consequences that are unacceptable in the longer run. Or it can be explained as a consequence of the new, high oil prices. Or as a mixture of the two. In either case it appears to policy makers as an external force with which they must learn to cope.

We live in a time when the living conditions of the world community are changing fast in many respects. These changes can often influence the ways in which the problems of inflation and unemployment present themselves. It is probably the unemployment problem that will be influenced most by external changes. Whether it be technological change, a new division of labor between rich and poor countries, or the transition to a period of slower economic growth, the main consequence will usually be a changed demand for certain types of labor. There can also be important changes in the relations between the demand for labor and capital.

The economic systems today do not easily adapt themselves to such changes appearing as influences coming from the outside. We are, therefore, faced with two types of problems: How can the economies be changed so as to avoid the internal disharmonies developing within the systems? How can they be changed so as to adapt themselves better to changes in their environment?

NO WAY BACK

It is tempting to ask the following question: If it is true that the economies have lost much of the self-adjusting capacity of former times, can we not go back to the old systems of the 19th century, when prices, wages, and employment moved up and down but never got locked in an extreme situation for any length of time?

There is no possibility of moving backward in history. Concentration of industry has been unavoidable because large enterprises are superior in branches where certain overhead costs, such as research and development, are important. The larger the market, the lower these costs per unit produced.

For the same reason multinational corporations and international banking operations were bound to expand. If larger markets are desirable, there must be a natural tendency to extend the activities to as many countries as possible.

Similarly, it could not be avoided that wage earners united more and more. If those who have products to sell gain strength by becoming bigger, the same must be true for those who have labor to sell.

Finally, the public sector has been bound to expand in modern societies. We live in what I have called, in *Development in Rich and Poor Countries*, "The Egalitarian Revolution." In order to reduce inequalities and make living conditions acceptable to everybody, the national states have taken the responsibility for education, health care, and other aspects of public welfare. Therefore, budgets have had to be large, and fiscal policy has become an important political issue. Monetary policy, too, became the responsibility of the public authorities because the old gold standard could not permit the circulation of money to be adjusted to the changing situations of modern societies.

If we cannot go back, we must go forward. We must accept that markets are organized, and increasingly so. And we must accept that the political authorities of national states have important roles to play, now supplemented by a number of international organizations.

The question is, therefore, how decision making in these private and public bodies can be coordinated so that the economies can function more harmoniously than they do today. The remaining parts of this chapter deal with various aspects of this problem.

TOWARD PRICE STABILITY AND FULL EMPLOYMENT

From the considerations above, it follows that the present difficulties have to do with the functioning of all three types of markets. If we are to come as close as possible to price stability and full employment, the performance of the product, labor, and capital markets must be modified. In this section we shall, therefore, look at these three types of markets separately.

Since inflation is one of the causes of unemployment, there is no easy solution that consists in accepting inflation while fighting unemployment. As a consequence, one should have both these problems in mind when reading the following discussion of the three categories of markets.

Demand management through the public sector will become easier if the performance of the various markets can be improved. Some remarks about the public sector will, therefore, conclude this section.

Product Markets

In the parts of the business sector where much of the production is concentrated in a few firms, those firms' price fixing can have both direct and indirect consequences of great importance. The direct consequence is that they can push prices upward and thus contribute to inflation. As mentioned earlier in this chapter, the firms can accept wage increases fairly easily, and thereby indirectly further inflation. Also, these wage increases may be too high for enterprises in the fields where there is more competition, the result being unemployment in these branches.

This is why price control has become an important policy issue. The weak point in present price control systems is, however, transnational pricing, in which prices are fixed in one country while the goods are sold in another. A country cannot really control prices fixed by firms in another country. And such price fixing is now a factor of growing importance.

One can distinguish between two problems in this field. There is, first, the case in which those who export have a strong market power, so that prices in the importing country are high. The country of the exporting firms can, of course, have a price control system that includes export prices, but often such prices are exempted from control. This is tempting because the country as a whole is interested in getting high prices for its exports.

The problem is especially complicated if the prices are fixed not by a single firm but by an export cartel comprising firms from several countries. Such cartels have been the subject of much international discussion. It has been recommended that there should at least be a notification of export cartels.[1] From an international point of view it is desirable that such cartels should not be exempted from price control, but it is not easy to bring about an agreement among all the countries involved. Some countries do, however, have legislation about export cartels.

The other main type of transnational price fixing is the transfer pricing of multinational corporations. This is an internal affair within the group of firms registered in various countries that, among themselves, form the multinational concern. Nevertheless, any price involved is fixed in an individual country and it depends on that country to what extent there is control. This case, too, is covered by a report from OECD that also has made recommendations concerning this matter.[2]

The most far-reaching measures concerning transnational price fixing have been taken by the European Communities, where restrictive practices that can prevent or limit competition are prohibited if they can influence trade between member countries. This important principle does not cover only cartels or other agreements between firms. It also covers the case where a single enterprise has a dominant position in the Common Market or substantial parts thereof, and if there is an abuse of this market power. Here we have the first example of international price control.

In view of the growing importance of transnational price fixing, it is desirable that such policies be extended to parts of the world other than the member countries of the European Communities. This will be a difficult task, but it should not be impossible to make some progress within the OECD area, where there are already recommendations about the possibility for member countries to get information from or request consultation with one another when it is considered desirable.

It would be a valuable step forward for the world economy as a whole if at least the major Western countries could agree on measures regarding price control similar to those of the European Communities. After all, these are the home countries of a large part of the export cartels and multinational corporations.

I have used the term "price control" instead of the somewhat broader concept "competition policy," which is used in the legislation of some countries. The term relates to American antitrust legislation and may, for instance, comprise measures against cartels or mergers of firms, thus trying to force enterprises to compete more than they otherwise would have done.

It is not necessary to discuss this wider concept here. It should be noted, though, that cooperation between firms, as well as mergers, can be part of a valuable rationalization of the industry in question. What is important, from the point of view of fighting inflation and unemployment, is to prevent firms with market power from abusing this power by charging unreasonable prices.

What is essential, therefore, is the control of prices, whether they are fixed in the country where the goods are sold or elsewhere. The control authorities must, of course, have information about the cost structure of the enterprises in question, and then decide how high the prices charged may be.

If this is done, the situation described in Figure 4.1 is changed. The new situation is outlined in Figure 6.1. It shows a firm with relatively strong market power, like the one shown in Figure 4.1.B. It has fixed a price, p_1, and the control authority decides that this price shall be lowered to p_2. As a consequence the quantity sold will rise from x_1 to x_2.

FIGURE 6.1: The Effect of Price Control

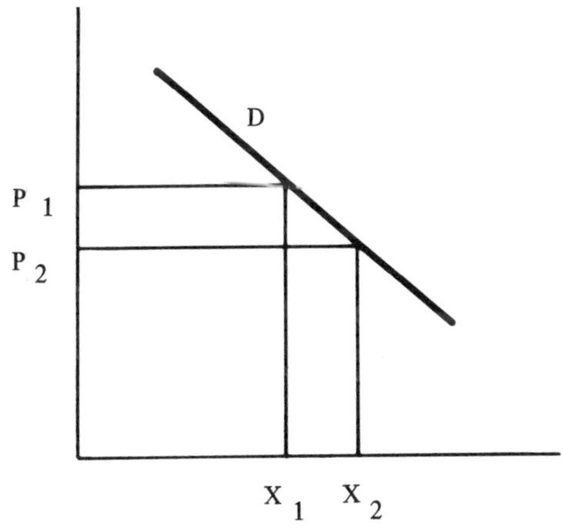

Source: Constructed by the author.

The situation of the firm now resembles that existing in a market where there is free or perfect competition. In both cases the price is something over which the seller has no influence. Whether this is the result of competition among many sellers or of a decision made by an authority is not important.

The most direct result of such price control is, of course, that some prices will be somewhat lower than they would have been otherwise. If efficient control is exercised, there will be a reduction in the rate of inflation. The enterprises whose prices are affected lose market power.

There also will be indirect consequences. As can be seen from the figure, sales will be increased. This means that there will be a reduction in unemployment because more can be produced. This, of course, is a reduction that takes place once and for all when the price is lowered; but if price control is maintained, the accumulated effect on inflation and employment may be substantial. Naturally, much depends on the scope of the control system, especially whether it comprises important parts of the product markets (including cases where prices are fixed in one country while the products are sold in another).

A particularly important indirect consequence of price control is the effect it can have on the fixing of wages. As mentioned earlier in this chapter, enterprises with market power can fairly easily accept wage rises because they can pass them on to consumers through higher prices. This, however, may not be so if there is efficient price control. The enterprises must then be careful regarding wages. This means that the price control system can act indirectly as a modifying impact on the tendencies of wages, as well as prices, to rise.

This being so, the control of prices can not only dampen inflation on a relatively broad front but also have an indirect effect on unemployment. One of the difficulties at present is that enterprises with strong market power can accept wage rises that are too high for those firms exposed to more competition. This is bound to have a negative influence on production and employment in the part of the economy that was called the competing sector in Chapters 3 and 4. That there is such a negative influence on employment in that sector can be seen clearly in Table 4.6.

Now, if price control eliminates the market power of enterprises where it is strong, wages will be lower and the sheltered and competing sectors of industry will be in approximately the same situation. Then the competing sector will not run the same risk as now of being forced to accept wages that are too high. As a consequence the present risk of unemployment in that sector will be reduced.

The above considerations are valid only where price control is efficient. To what extent that is true in the various countries is not easy to judge. Price control is by no means an easy task. The authorities are not able to get as much understanding of the situation of enterprises as it would be desirable to have before a decision is made. It should not be forgotten that if the prices ordered by the authorities are too low, part of the production may be given up, with some unemployment resulting.

The main problem in the years to come will, however, be to make some progress toward an internationalization of price control.

Labor Markets

The labor market is a particularly important element of a national economic system. In modern societies wages are usually on the order of 60 to 70 percent of GNP. The price of labor is, therefore, by far the most important of all prices. It is, in fact, the dominant factor in the price system.

At the same time labor-market problems are politically among the most difficult parts of an economic policy. Wage earners are the great majority of the population in a modern society, often between 80 and 90 percent of the age groups active in the labor market. Traditionally they have been looked at as the poorer part of the nation, and some of them still belong to the low-income groups.

On the other hand, it is one of the main results of the analysis undertaken in this book that the present functioning of the labor and product markets is the chief cause of the existing combination of inflation and unemployment. In the interplay between those two markets, labor has, on the whole, had the upper hand, as can be seen from Chapter 4 and especially from Table 4.5.

It follows that since prices must be controlled where there is market power, the same is true of wages. This does not mean that the methods can be the same in these two cases. There are substantial differences.

Prices are fixed by the enterprise that sells the products. If the prices are considered too high compared with the costs of production, the control authorities can order that they be lowered. Wages, on the other hand, are mostly fixed by collective bargaining between two parties. There are no costs of production to be compared with the price of labor. If the authorities are to intervene, or only to counsel, the intervention or counsel must, therefore, be based on reasoning of a more general nature.

The problems regarding the labor markets are, thus, complicated. This being so, and because of their unique importance, I have found it useful in the discussion below to divide these problems into four groups.

Procedures

In price control the authorities can simply order an enterprise to lower its prices, if they are considered too high. As regards wages the procedures are more complicated. Government has a role to play, but collective bargaining deals not only with wages but also with working hours, working conditions, and other subjects. As a consequence, most of the details of the agreements to be reached must be handled by the labor-market organizations. Finally, many decisions concerning wages and working conditions are made at the enterprise level. Decision making, thus, takes place at three levels, which makes the procedures complicated.

The role of government usually will be to formulate guidelines, which may be concentrated around the central question in any wage negotiation: Can wages be allowed to rise, and if so, by how much? It may, of course, be necessary for the guidelines to be more specific, dealing with problems other than the general trend of wages.

The guidelines to be defined by government often will be based on an analysis of the economy undertaken by government advisers. It also may be useful for the political authorities to discuss relevant problems with the labor-market organizations at intervals. The attitude of labor unions may well be influenced by the prospects concerning taxation, employment, the cost of living, and so on.

It may be tempting for governments to play no role at all in these delicate problems, leaving them to the organizations. But the analysis made in this book strongly indicates that if market mechanisms continue to function as they do at present in most modern societies, we are bound to have both inflation and unemployment in the foreseeable future. The fixing of wages is, therefore, a political problem.

The role of the organizations in the fixing of wages should, of course, be as great as possible. If they can reach an informal agreement with the political authorities on the general level that is permissible, it is desirable that the negotiations be carried out by the organizations. This can most easily be the case in countries where organization is centralized to a fairly high degree on both sides.

It is important that the organizations of employers and wage earners be able to explain the reasoning behind the settlement aimed at to their members. Often it can be difficult to convince many wage earners that restraint in the fixing of wages is necessary in order to reduce unemployment.

The relations between the income levels of various groups of workers and employees also can become the subject of difficult discussions within the organizations. If a certain group of wage earners feels that advantages given to other groups have been harmful to their own relative position, they may be eager to ask for similar advantages, thus starting a movement toward a general wage rise. The organizations can play a constructive role by discussing such questions with representatives of the groups concerned in time to avoid a disruption of the realistic development of wages that must be aimed at in the general negotiations.

It is also a possibility that more general political questions regarding, say, taxation or the protection of workers may be raised in connection with wage negotiations. It is, therefore, desirable that the organizations of both employers and wage earners be in contact with the political authorities now and then to be informed about the prospects in various fields. In democratic societies it is desirable that there be the highest possible degree of consensus in the population regarding strategic decisions like those of a wage policy.

As mentioned above, some of the decisions concerning wages are made at the enterprise level. This is especially the case when the rates agreed upon in collective bargaining are minimum wages. In that case additions can be decided on when a firm hires workers. The labor market is still, to some extent, a free market.

The wage drift is a result of this multitude of decisions made at the enterprise level. It is, as a general rule, increasing when a country approaches full employment, because enterprises must then compete more keenly for qualified labor than when there is more unemployment. The imperfect mobility of the labor force has, however, created a situation where this competition can pull wages upward even when many people are unemployed.

There often will be a danger that a wage drift can undermine the results of the general wage negotiations for the country as a whole. It is, therefore, desirable that enterprises have guidance from the organizations to which they belong, so that this can be avoided.

It also is worth considering whether in some cases it would be preferable that the general wage level for certain categories of labor was fixed as a norm and not as a minimum. This would mean that deviations agreed upon at the enterprise level could be downward as well as upward. In the section "Adjustment to Changes" below, it will be argued that we need more flexibility than we have today in order to avoid unemployment when the situation of a certain branch is changing fast.

A Wage Policy

What should be the contents, or at least the general principles, of a realistic wage policy, for which the government has the main responsibility?

It is important that the initial position be realistic. If the cost level of a country is too high compared with those of its main competitors, it means that the exchange rate of the country's currency is overestimated. It follows that if this exchange rate is maintained, wages should be reduced in order to make the country more competitive, but that is hardly feasible in societies of today.

It is, therefore, desirable that in such a case the exchange rate should be lowered so as to correspond to the real situation of the country before a general round of wage negotiations begins. The importance of making exchange rates concordant with the situation of the country without waiting too long has been stressed by an experienced adviser to the IMF, Jacques J. Polak, in his lecture at the Per Jacobsson Foundation in 1979.[3] Dr. Polak summarizes his observations on this important subject in the following conclusion: "No country has an advantage in sticking to a disequilibrium rate for its currency, and no country in the end manages to do so."

If the exchange rate has been lowered before a wage negotiation, it is essential that the results of the devaluation not be lost by new wage rises that again make the cost level too high. It is not an easy task to ensure that this is avoided, because the devaluation will raise the cost of living somewhat.

If we now assume that the starting situation is a realistic one, what, as a general rule, can be the average change of wages allowed during the period covered by the agreement? It is tempting to answer that wages can be raised by the same percentage as the increase in what is usually called the productivity of labor. This would, however, not be a realistic assumption to start with.

Production is the result of the working together of various factors of production. One cannot therefore, in the true sense of the word talk about the productivity of one of these factors, as if it could be seen in isolation. Labor alone could produce only in the simple ways known by our forefathers before the rise of agriculture and domestic animals some 10,000 years ago. Capital alone can produce nothing at all. Thus, only a combination of the two factors is meaningful today.

It is, therefore, impossible to tell how much of the production today is the result of labor and how much is the result of capital. Theoretically, one could ask how much production could increase if a certain quantity of labor was added while the input of capital was not increased. Or one could ask how much production would rise if a certain amount of capital was added while the quantity of labor was unchanged. No general answer to such questions can be given, though similar calculations are made when enterprises are planning their work.

It was shown in Chapters 3 and 4 that in recent decades this planning has led to the investment of more and more capital per working hour. Also, more and more fixed labor costs have been added because of the large salaried staffs of modern enterprises (see in particular Table 3.2).

One of the main results of the analysis undertaken in Chapters 3 and 4 is that the increase of production in recent decades has to a large extent been due to increased investment and to other overhead expenditure, such as research and development. But nobody can say even approximately how much of the additional production has been made possible by these particular inputs. Nor, as a consequence, is it possible to say which part of the production is due to the input of ordinary labor.

The growth of productivity in the recent past, therefore, gives us no guidance as to the annual rise of wages that would be compatible with a future satisfactory development. What we know is that profits have represented a declining part of the results of industry (see Tables 3.2 and 4.5). If, nevertheless, it has been profitable to invest more and more capital per worker employed, it is because the real price of capital has become lower and lower because of inflation—and even negative for many investors.

Labor has, thus, become more and more expensive compared with capital. This is why it has increasingly been replaced by capital, the result being growing unemployment. It was shown in Table 4.3 that in the period covered by the table, real wages increased in roughly the same proportion as what is, somewhat superficially, called labor productivity. But this has been a period of growing inflation and, since the late 1960s, also of growing unemployment. If any general conclusion is to be drawn from the above considerations, it must be that future wage rises should, compared with labor productivity growth, be lower than in the past. Nobody can say how much lower.

We cannot even say how much this labor productivity will grow in the future. I will come back to this question in the section "Adjustment to Changes." It is worth noting, however, that, as mentioned in Chapter 5, the annual growth of labor productivity may have to be only 2.0 percent per year until 1990, compared with 4.5 percent per year in 1960-73.

This is a drastic decline of productivity growth. It indicates that if we are to approach full employment during the 1980s, the annual wage rises in the West will, on the average, have to be so much lower than in the recent past that we can talk about a new period, radically different from the preceding one.

The estimates represented by the above figures are, of course, fairly uncertain, but the latest development does not seem to indicate that they are on the pessimistic side as far as economic growth is concerned. We should be prepared for a difficult period of transition to a changed pattern of development.

The first conclusion to be drawn from the above considerations is that it is not possible to define any growth rate for wages that will be the ideal one for a certain country. Too much depends on unknown factors, and much depends on how strong the political will to move toward price stability and full employment is in the country in question.

If there is a second general conclusion to be drawn, it is that one should aim at a wage development that brings the country as close as possible to price stability. This will also be beneficial to employment, but it is difficult to estimate to what extent and how fast.

A particular aspect of a wage policy is the attitude to take vis-à-vis the efforts to obtain an equalization of wages. If wages in some of the low-wage groups are raised in order to bring them closer to those of the better-paid categories of labor, there is a risk of two undesired effects.

One is that there can be unemployment in the groups whose wages are raised. If the price of these categories of simple labor becomes higher, the work usually done by such people may cease to be done because it is considered too expensive. This is why housemaids have nearly disappeared in the rich countries, as have a number of other personal services.

The other consequence is that employers prefer more qualified people when the wage differentials are reduced without a corresponding reduction in the quality differentials. This also means unemployment for some of those whose wages are raised but it also means that wages of the more qualified categories of workers are pulled upward because of the increased demand. This, in turn, will increase the demand for still more qualified labor, which is now relatively cheaper than before.

In this way the wage rise can spread upward through the labor market, the result being more inflation and nearly no relative improvement for the groups that were to be helped. Experience in Denmark has confirmed that efforts to enforce equalization of wages can have such effects.

It must, of course, be added that if there is a gradual equalization of qualifications because the general standards of education and training are raised, it is natural that this should lead to a corresponding narrowing of the gaps within the wage system. What should be avoided is only that the wages of certain groups are pushed upward so fast that demand for them is reduced or transferred to other groups.

Mobility of Labor

In economic literature it has been customary to talk about frictional unemployment when there are vacant jobs and unemployed persons at the same time because these persons do not know where the vacant jobs are, or because they cannot easily move to the places where the jobs are. These problems are not serious today because of the modern means of communication and transport. It is easy to spread information about available jobs and it is possible to have a fairly long distance between one's home and one's place of work.

Rapid technological and other changes have, however, created a new problem that is not easy to tackle without modifications of the economic systems. New types of jobs are being created all the time, and other types of jobs are disappearing or having their numbers reduced. This being so, it is possible that there can be quite many vacant jobs and unemployed persons at the same time. This is sometimes called technological unemployment. It is, however, related to the old frictional unemployment because it has to do with a certain lack of mobility. It is not surprising that rapid change raises the need for mobility of the labor force.

This new type of unemployment raises three policy questions: 1. Are the unemployed persons willing to take the available jobs? 2. Are they allowed to do so? 3. Are they qualified to do so?

The first has to do with the system of unemployment compensation. This system has changed much in recent years in most modern societies. Sometimes the level of unemployment compensation is not much lower than the wages a person can get in a new job. The incentive to take a new job may not be strong if the available job is fairly different from the former one. Much, therefore, depends on the rules in force in the particular country. Can a worker refuse the job and continue to receive unemployment compensation? Such rules are probably on the whole more liberal than in former times.

Higher levels of compensation and more liberal rules have made the situation of an unemployed person more acceptable. It cannot be denied, however, that such changes can also weaken the inclination to look for a job and to accept a job if one can be found.

There is a third change in the system that is more fundamental. Originally unemployment insurance was much more of a real insurance system in most countries than it is today. Now it is customary for the public sector to pay most of the costs of the system. This means that the wage earners or—more generally—the bargaining parties are not made directly responsible for the unemployment that may be created if wages are fixed at a level that is too high.

This is an important problem. It can be seen from the analysis undertaken in this book that wages have been raised to such an extent that both inflation and unemployment have resulted. This also has to do with market power in parts of the product markets and with the ways in which liquidity has been made available in the capital markets. It remains that wage rises have played a major role, and in most countries the fixing of wages has to a large extent been the responsibility of the two parties in the collective bargaining.

If the mobility of labor is to be increased, the rules concerning unemployment compensation should not make it too easy to refuse a job and yet continue to receive support from the system. It would also make the labor unions more directly responsible for unemployment if the system could again be transformed into a real insurance system. The unions would then have an interest in finding jobs for their members and getting the members to accept these jobs. It also might be a good idea to let employers pay part of the premiums so that they too would feel a direct responsibility for the maintenance of employment. This is done in some countries.

Such changes would reintroduce some of the old self-adjusting forces into the labor markets. Requests for wage rises would be more cautious because increased unemployment would mean higher premiums in the insurance system. And unions would, more directly than now, be interested in the mobility of labor and in a reduction of unemployment.

The above considerations deal only with the first of the three questions connected with mobility—the interest of the unemployed in seeking and accepting available jobs. The second question—Are they allowed to take these jobs?—raises a different kind of problem.

The structure of the labor movement is, for obvious reasons, marked by historical traditions. Each union usually represents a special type of work, such as one of the old handicrafts. In modern societies the nature of many jobs is, however, changing fast and new types of jobs are being created. This makes it desirable that a person who has become unemployed be allowed to take a new job, even if it belongs to a field under the jurisdiction of a labor union to which that worker does not belong. This would in several cases imply a relaxation of the system of labor unions. Members of a certain union would have to accept new members who do not have the same kind of training as the old members. And they would be exposed to competition from these new members, which in some cases might make it more difficult to raise the level of wages.

The changes suggested above would not be easy for labor unions to accept. They would, however, tend to reduce unemployment and, thus, be helpful to union members who would otherwise be without jobs. These changes should, incidentally, be seen in a wider context. It will be argued in the next section that a new labor/management relationship is under way and that this tendency should be furthered. This will, in the long run, change the position of workers and employees and modify labor unions' concepts and their ideas about the purposes for which they have to work.

It remains to discuss the third question that was raised in connection with the problem of labor mobility: Will workers who are unemployed be qualified to take the available jobs they might be able to find? In many cases they will not be qualified immediately. They must, therefore, be retrained. This retraining often will take place on the job, in the enterprise where the person in question has become a member of the staff. Many enterprises have their own training systems that enable them to give their workers and employees exactly the skills that are needed.

There is, however, a more general problem that is relevant for society as a whole. Many modern jobs are highly specialized, and so are many systems of training and education. But a high degree of specialization can be an obstacle to mobility. In a rapidly changing world, many kinds of education are becoming partly obsolete within a fairly short span of time. Another difficulty is that people who have been trained or educated in a very specific way may find that after a few years they must change occupation and start a new type of work for which their education is not relevant.

It should, therefore, be considered whether it would not be preferable to make at least some of the professional educational systems less specialized. We should educate people in such ways that they can change occupation more easily than many specialists can today.

There is an enormous fund of knowledge available in the world, and it is growing all the time. Nobody can perceive more than a very limited part of this knowledge. The question is, thus, what should be the nature of this part. If it is within a very specialized field, the person in question acquires the capacity to do something very specific and nothing else. On the contrary, a person who gets a more general education may be better qualified for change. He or she may then be able to acquire some specific knowledge later on, if it is desirable in the job held or looked for. If he or she changes jobs, it may be possible to acquire new, specific knowledge of a different kind.

In our changing world there is a need for lifelong learning. We must adapt ourselves to new knowledge that is being created. This being so, it can be a waste of intellectual resources for many people to get a long, very specific education. We must, of course, have specialists in many fields, but we also must have people who can change occupations without too much difficulty. It deserves serious consideration how the educational systems can be modified so as to strengthen people's capacity to change.

Labor/Management Relationships

The distribtuion of wealth and power has been subject to changes throughout history. In medieval Europe landed property was the main source of wealth, and the big landowners became a dominant class. They did, however, share the power with the clergy, which had the spiritual leadership.

With the emergence of industry, capital became a dominant factor of production. The captains of industry were powerful both as managers and as owners of capital. No wonder the system was called "capitalism" by the socialist authors who reacted against the inequalities of that period.

But society continued to change. Political power has gradually been transferred to the people as a whole. In the economic systems two major changes have taken place. The ownership of capital is no longer as concentrated as it was in the 19th century, and the dominant influence in industry depends less and less on the ownership of capital.

Thanks to the modern financial system, capital can be invested in very large enterprises and, thus, become more concentrated. At the same time, the ownership of this capital can be spread more and more. It can belong to many thousands of people who own stocks, bonds, or deposits in banks and savings banks, even if we consider only the capital invested in a single enterprise. The managers of the large enterprises may or may not be important stockholders, but increasingly they are people who have their position because they are considered competent, not because they have capital.

In the 20th century even the power of management is beginning to be spread. Representatives of workers and employees are increasingly taking part in decision making in modern enterprises. Democracy is spreading from the political to the economic system. The latest feature of this development is a tendency to give workers and employees a part of the profits and/or the ownership of capital of the enterprises.

A number of such systems exist, and others have been discussed in various countries.[4] The existing systems are voluntary, with the exception of a French arrangement, which is compulsory for enterprises with more than 100 persons employed. Compulsory systems have been proposed in the Netherlands and Denmark, but no legislation has so far been carried through. The establishment of voluntary systems has been encouraged through tax incentives in various countries.

If such systems of participation in profits and in the ownership of enterprises were to spread, it would represent a continuation of the general trends mentioned above. Both the ownership of capital and decision making in enterprises have been spread to some extent, but the most important decisions are still made at general meetings, where those who control more than half of the owned capital can dominate. And profits are earned by those who have parts of the owned capital.

These trends are mentioned here because they may influence the attitudes of wage earners in the difficult discussions about wage restraint and mobility of labor that can be expected in the years to come. They also may influence the attitudes of labor unions, and in many countries they may influence political parties that have traditional links with the labor movement. It should not be forgotten that though incomes policy has been a subject for discussion since the 1960s, no country has yet had a really successful wage policy.

It is a main result of the analysis made in this book that labor has been in a strong position in recent decades. Profits have gone down, and even in branches where enterprises have had strong market power, much of the results have been transferred to labor through wage rises.

If there is now to be much more restraint in the fixing of wages, does it mean that labor will lose what it has gained, sometimes by fighting hard? Will profits rise again, at the expense of labor? Shall labor, in addition, take over most of the financing of unemployment compensation, now largely covered by the public sector? And shall the rules regarding such compensation be made more restrictive?

Such questions are not easy to answer. And even if it can be generally agreed that one of the purposes is to reduce unemployment, nobody can tell how many more workers will be employed if a certain claim for a wage rise is reduced from, say, 6 to 2 percent. These questions are difficult because they are aspects of the more general problem of the distribution of income in society. Though this distribution is much less unequal now than in the 19th century, there is still a fairly high degree of inequality in many countries.

To this must be added that the distribution of power is even more unequal. The spread of decision making in enterprises has been valuable, but the real power concerning the most essential problems is, as a rule, still highly concentrated. In a large multinational corporation working in many countries, the power may be in the hands of a small group of persons who control the majority of stock in the parent company.

Implicitly, all the questions mentioned above are aspects of the old conflict between capital and labor. This conflict has led to a socialist revolution in some countries. That has been avoided in the West because there has been a gradual transition to societies with less inequality than in the past. It remains, however, to be said that the two parties in collective bargaining are still the representatives of capital and labor. And now, in the fight against inflation and unemployment, the representatives of labor are asked to show more restraint. Will they get anything in return?

It is at this crucial point that the problem of wage-earner participation in profits and in the owned capital of enterprises comes up. If wage restraint leads to higher profits, the workers and employees will get a share of this gain if there is a system of profit sharing. And if the system implies that they also get an increasing part of the owned capital, as has been proposed in some countries, they also will have a say on the board of directors and at the stockholders' meeting.

There is a long way to go before wage earners in most Western countries have a substantial influence in the business sector through such participation. In some countries they have a dominant influence in many enterprises through voluntary arrangements, but what are the possibilities for more widespread systems of participation?

They are probably greater than is generally recognized. Because wage earners are now the great majority of the population in modern societies, and because of the spread of capital ownership referred to above, wage earners now own much capital. As a consequence they are able to acquire much owned capital if they are interested in getting influence in this way.

Table 6.1 shows the distribution of the ownership of capital among persons in Denmark, a small, typical modern society. It will be seen that the wage earners own more capital than the entrepreneurs. The pensioners include former entrepreneurs, but increasingly they will be former wage earners. Among the employees there are, of course, presidents of large companies, but also many persons of other ranks, (see Table 4.1).

A large part of the stocks and other assets in the country is owned by corporations, including banks, but directly or indirectly the owned capital of enterprises is held by persons. The table shows that, if they so desire, wage earners can acquire much owned capital of enterprises in the years to come.

It can be expected that the problems regarding voluntary and compulsory systems of worker participation in profits and in owned capital of enterprises will be the subject of lively discussions in several countries. It is desirable that further progress should be made in this field. This would gradually break down the barriers between capitalists and workers because more and more people would become a combination of both. And that would make it easier for them to see the problems of the labor markets in a wider perspective.

Capital Markets

It is essential that real rates of interest shall be made positive again for all investors as soon as possible. As long as they are

TABLE 6.1: Ownership of Capital in Denmark, 1974

	Stocks, etc. (billion kr.)	*All Assets (billion kr.)*	*Liabilities (billion kr.)*	*Net Wealth (billion kr.)*
Entrepreneurs	1.5	119.7	65.2	54.5
Employees	3.8	117.1	66.1	51.0
Workers	0.5	60.9	32.1	28.8
Pensioners	2.1	67.0	8.9	58.1
Others	0.5	6.1	3.8	2.3
Total	8.4	370.8	176.1	194.7

Note: 1 krone = U.S. $0.18.

Source: Lonmodtagernes Medejendomsret, "Report by a Commission on Workers' Participation," (Copenhagen: 1978), p. 259.

negative, too much capital will be invested in labor saving machinery and equipment. The pattern of investment will therefore continue to be harmful to employment. As explained earlier, the main reason why real rates of interest are negative for most investors in many countries is inflation. Interest and repayment of loans can be paid with money that is worth less and less compared with the money one has borrowed.

The main instruments for fighting against inflation are the policies concerning price control and wage fixing described in the two previous sections. It will, however, take quite a long time before these policies have become really efficient in most countries. Can anything be done in the meantime in order to avoid an excess of labor saving investment? Borrowing for investment naturally depends on the situation in the capital markets too. If ample liquidity is available on easy terms, labor saving investment can be financed without difficulty.

It was stressed in Chapter 3 that though rising rates of inflation tend to provoke rising rates of interest, this correlation is only imperfect. Therefore, even after a long period of high rates of inflation, nominal rates of interest will not have increased correspondingly. As a consequence, real rates of interest tend to be negative in many cases. This is illustrated by Table 3.4. Of the eight countries covered by the table, the first four have low rates of inflation, and their interest rates are substantially higher than the inflation rates, so the real rates of interest are positive, as they should be.

The last four countries in the table have high rates of inflation, but their interest rates have not adjusted to this situation. In France the real rate of interest is about 0; in the other three countries it is negative. It is likely that the real rate of interest after taxes is negative for most investors in these four countries.

This, of course, has to do with monetary policy, and in this field substantial changes have taken place. In the old days of the gold standard, the central bank would raise the bank rate when the gold stock began to decline because the balance of payments was negative. Higher rates of interest would then attract capital from abroad and also dampen economic activity in the country, thus bringing about a reduction of imports. If the gold stock was increasing, the bank rate would be lowered, with the opposite effects.

In the modern paper money systems, the situation in the capital markets depends more on policy decisions made by the governments or the central banks. There has been a tendency to pay less attention to the rates of interest and more to the quantity of money. This is the main conclusion of a report from OECD.[5] After a review of recent discussions and of the practices of the major OECD member countries, it is concluded that countries should define and publicize targets for the growth of the money or credit aggregates that would be allowed to develop. This should stabilize the expectations about inflation and reduce the risk of ever higher inflation rates.

This does not look convincing. The rates of inflation in the OECD area have been high in recent years; and after a small reduction in 1978, when the real price of oil fell, they started rising again in 1979 and 1980. The direct effect of the oil price rises can explain only part of this inflation.

That is not surprising. It is a main result of the analysis of this book that the present type of inflation is primarily a price/cost-push inflation. The active force has been the growing market power of enterprises and labor unions. The growth of the money stocks has, on the whole, been a passive adaptation to the growing money value of transactions in countries with rising prices and wages. It follows that a definition of the growth rates of the money stocks to be allowed does not attack the present type of inflation at its roots.

This does not mean that there is no need for control in the capital markets. What it means is that the rates of interest should play a greater role in monetary policy than they do today. There is a relationship between quantity and price in capital markets, as in other markets. If the quantity of money in a country is increased, prices (that is, interest rates) tend to fall. If the prices are raised, the quantity of capital demanded tends to fall. One can, therefore, influence capital markets both by altering the quantity of money available and by changing interest rates.

The difference is that if the policy consists of fixing a target for the growth of the money stock, such a target must be based on guesswork. One may assume, for instance, that production will increase by 3 percent the following year and that the rate of inflation will be 8 percent. In that case the money stock must be allowed to increase by 11.2 percent (1.03 x 1.08 = 1.112). Both these estimates are uncertain, and so is any estimate of the velocity of money circulation. If money circulates faster than before, the same stock of money can finance transactions at higher prices. And if economic growth should happen to be only 2 percent instead of 3, the projected money stock can finance a rate of inflation of 9 percent instead of 8.

If, on the other hand, the monetary policy is based primarily on aiming at a certain interest level, market mechanisms can play a greater role and one is not bound to finance predetermined rates of inflation. In this case the central bank also will have to make decisions that will influence the size of the stock of money, but it can proceed by trial and error.

To illustrate that, we may choose an example taken from Table 3.4. In the last part of 1979 the rate of inflation in the United States was 12.7 percent and the long-term rate of interest was 11.35 percent. Let us assume that the intention was to make the real rate of interest positive by aiming at a long-term interest rate of, say, 14 percent in the near future. Other things being equal, this would require the central bank system to sell bonds in order to depress their prices and thereby increase the effective rate of interest. Such sales would bring money into the central bank system and thus reduce the circulating money stock.

But other things are not equal. Production is increasing or decreasing at a certain rate, and the rate of inflation is high. There may be a desire to dampen this inflation somehow, and though this is primarily a question of price and wage control, it also is important to ensure that the level of total demand is not too high. There also may be a public deficit to finance and a desire to improve the balance of payments.

These and other considerations will have to decide how the stock of money can be allowed to develop. One should, therefore, not be bound by a target. If a target has been set in advance, it should be subject to revision at any time.

It is tempting to object that higher interest rates would be harmful to investment and, therefore, also to economic growth and to employment. But this kind of reasoning would be off the mark. We will have to approach full employment with relatively low rates of economic growth, as shown in the last section of Chapter 5. This speaks against a very capital-intensive type of development. It can be added that in the West investment as a percentage of GNP has been remarkably stable since 1961, in spite of changing rates of growth. These percentages have been as shown below.[6]

Years	*Industrialized Countries*	*Developing Countries*
1961-65	21.9	20.0
1966-74	22.1	21.3
1975-77	21.6	24.5

Note: Industrialized countries are the OECD area, minus Southern Europe plus South Africa.

That investment has increased in developing countries corresponds to the fact that the South has speeded up economic growth and industrialization, as shown in Chapter 5. In the West investment culminated in 1974, when projects started before the first oil price rise were finished. In 1975-77 considerable investment was made in oil drilling.

In order to increase the demand for labor in the years to come, the price relationship between labor and capital must be changed. Labor must become cheaper compared with capital. This is why a restraint on wage development should be combined with a capital market policy that makes the real rates of interest positive, and increasingly so.

Because of the modern organization of capital markets described in Chapter 2, capital is now flowing easily between countries. This has increased the interdependence, especially of Western countries, as regards interest rates. If rates are increased in one country and not in others, the first country will attract capital from the others. It follows that if we are to have more clearly defined interest rate policies, coordination between the leading Western countries will be needed. The policy of the United States in this field is particularly important because interest rate behavior in the Eurodollar market is similar to what it is in the U.S. market.[7]

The Eurodollar market is part of the private international capital markets that have developed in the postwar period. Fear has been expressed that this may contribute to an overexpansion of liquidity. The question about the desirability of control over the international financial system has, therefore, been discussed.[8] This might facilitate the transition to the more deliberate interest rate policies mentioned above.

The Public Sector

In many countries it will be difficult to guide the public sector in the foreseeable future. Serious efforts must be made to come much closer to price stability and full employment. This must be done while economic growth is likely to be substantially slower than in the years before 1973, and most oil-importing countries will have balance-of-payments problems.

How, under such circumstances, shall the public sector be managed? It is not possible to draw up any general rules, but a few considerations may be appropriate. Since a few oil-exporting countries are bound to have a large balance-of-payments surplus for many years to come, the rest of the world is bound to have a corresponding deficit. The West is likely to have a large part of this deficit, and may even be under moral pressure to cover a larger part than today of the deficit in the poorest countries of the South. It is part of the problem that the West as a whole will have increasing debts on which interest must be paid.

This situation must be accepted. There is no point in creating a situation where each Western country tries to improve its balance of payments at the expense of other Western countries. This might easily happen, since nearly 70 percent of all the imports of Western countries come from other Western countries.

It would be desirable, after contacts between the West and OPEC, to make a rough estimate of the total Western balance-of-payments deficit for a number of years to come. After that, Western countries might discuss a reasonable distribution of this deficit among themselves.

Perhaps it is too optimistic to believe that something of the sort can be done, but it would in no way be meaningless to make an effort. If country A is to have an average balance-of-payments deficit of, say $2 billion a year during the 1980s, it would do harm both to this country and to others if it tried to obtain a surplus through restrictive policies.

The second-best solution would be for each country, on its own, to make an estimate of what might be a reasonable balance-of-payments deficit for some years to come. This estimate could serve as a guideline for demand management during that period.

At this point reference should be made to the discussion of related problems in Chapter 3, especially the section "Demand Management" and Figure 3.1. The conclusion to be drawn from this analysis is that as long as markets function as they do today, great changes in demand management can be dangerous. If more expansionary fiscal policies are pursued, there will be more inflation and employment may fairly soon cease to improve. If contractionary policies are then pursued, there will be more unemployment and inflation may continue almost as before.

The need for the political authorities to be involved in the fixing of wages has been discussed in a previous section. There is reason to repeat, however, that the public sector is the largest employer in most modern societies. The fixing of wages in that sector is, thus, a direct responsibility of the government. If public wages and salaries are fixed too low compared with those in the private sector, it is likely that there will be unrest. If they are too high, this is likely to influence private wages in the same direction. There is no escape for the political authorities from involvement in the general problem of a wage policy.

One final problem should be mentioned. Because of unemployment and economic difficulties for private enterprises, the public sector has become involved in various problems regarding the business sector. The involvement can take the form of protection against foreign competition or it can consist of subsidies, loans to enterprises, or the taking over of corporate stocks.

Whatever it may be, it is essential to make an evaluation of the real situation as soon as possible. Will the enterprise have to be closed down in a few years' time, or will it continue to be a losing concern? The main question in such cases usually will be whether, by supporting the enterprise, the public sector has postponed an unavoidable adjustment to the changed circumstances. Much may be at stake in a large enterprise, and it is tempting to postpone a decision to close it down.

Such problems, of which there are many today, have to do with the capacity of modern societies to adjust to change. This is the subject of the next section.

ADJUSTMENT TO CHANGE

In a rapidly changing world it is an important question how the economic systems can adjust to changes in the circumstances under which they will have to work. For obvious reasons this has much to do with the unemployment problem, since changing conditions of production can reduce or increase the demand for work. It has been mentioned in Chapter 4, the section "Reactions to Change," and in this chapter, the subsection "Mobility of Labor." In this section the purpose will be to discuss the problems in a more general way.

Changing External Conditions

Two changes in the external conditions were discussed in Chapter 4: technological change and changes in the division of labor between rich and poor countries. Other examples are the rising oil prices and the growing concern about the environment that has led to legislation about the use of certain materials. There is also the possibility of prices of certain raw materials rising compared with prices in general.

This latter question has been studied by The Economist Intelligence Unit.[9] The main conclusion is that raw material prices are likely to rise for two reasons. One is that there can be increasing costs of extraction because the materials are in remote areas or exist only in low concentration. The other is that processing of the materials is done increasingly in less-developed countries, where wages are low, so that the prices of the raw materials can come closer to those of the finished products.

In all these cases the conditions of production are changing. New combinations of labor and capital are called for in order to adapt the patterns of products and of methods of work to the new situation. These problems are sometimes more complicated as regards capital than they are as regards labor. Investment is an irreversible process. Once a factory with costly machinery has been built, the capital invested may be lost if it cannot be used. There has been a systematic closure of steelworks in some European countries in recent years. In other cases new investment can adapt the building, and perhaps part of the equipment, to the new situation.

As regards labor, it is always a question of a reduction of demand in some cases and/or an increase in other cases. The problems concerning the mobility of labor raised in this way have been discussed in another section of this chapter. But it may be added here that the situation may be complicated by the immobility of capital and of some natural resources. If an automobile factory is closed down because the oil price rises have reduced the demand for its products, the same price rises will have increased the demand for oil drilling. But the new jobs thus created will not be in the city of the factory, perhaps not even in the same country. There is no simple answer to the questions raised in this way. If new activities are to be started, an effort can be made to have them established in places where there is much unemployed labor, but this may require subsidies for retraining and perhaps for the reconstruction of buildings.

The adaptation to changing external conditions can be facilitated if one is prepared for them in time. Long-term planning in industry and in public institutions can be helpful in this respect. It may also be useful for labor unions to be involved in such attempts at forecasting. It is particularly important to stress that even the prospects of a rather specialized branch may be understood only if they are seen in the wider context of the development of society as a whole, perhaps even in a global perspective.

Lower Rates of Growth

In 1979 unemployment in the OECD area was about 5.1 percent. It would be a modest desire that it should be reduced to 2 percent in 1990. If this goal is to be attained, a comparison of the 1980s with the years of rapid growth, 1960-73, will be as follows: There will be a need for a more rapid growth of employment in a period when economic growth is likely to be substantially slower than in the past.

According to OECD estimates, the labor force of the area grew by 1.0 percent per year in 1960-75 and is expected to grow by 1.2 percent per year in 1975-90.[10] This increase in the growth rate is due to higher participation rates for women and to reduced emigration from some member countries. As shown in Figure 1.2, unemployment in 1973 was almost the same as in 1960. We can, therefore, suppose that employment in 1960-73 grew by 1.0 percent per year.

We can assume that during the 1980s the labor force will grow by 1.2 percent per year. If unemployment is to be reduced from 5.1 percent in 1979 to 2 percent in 1990, employment will have to increase by about 1.5 percent per year—substantially faster than in 1960-73.

According to OECD statistics the growth of GNP was 5.5 percent per year in the period 1960-73. As for the future, the OECD expert group that produced the report *Interfutures* made various scenarios for the future.[11] The one considered most likely to be true assumed a growth rate of 3.4 percent per year for 1975-2000. For 1975-90 the estimate was slightly higher: 3.6 percent per year.

The work on this project was, however, finished at the end of 1978. After the very large oil price rises in 1979-80, a corresponding estimate would probably be somewhat lower. If we assume that the growth rate for the 1980s will be 3.5 percent, it may therefore be on the optimistic side.

On the assumptions indicated above, we would get the following annual growth rates:

1960-73	*Percent*
GNP	5.5
Employment	1.0
Labor productivity	4.5

1980-90	*Percent*
GNP	3.5
Employment	1.5
Labor productivity	2.0

Labor productivity is here defined as production per unit of labor.

As mentioned in previously the term "labor productivity" is somewhat misleading because production is the combined result of the inputs of labor and capital. It also has been shown in Chapter 4 that the high rates of economic growth in the earlier period can, to a large extent, be explained by the high rates of investment increase that made production more and more capital-intensive. This allowed production per working hour to grow fast.

The figures above indicate that in this respect a drastic change can be expected. If labor productivity is to grow by only 2.0 percent per year instead of 4.5 percent, the pattern of development will be very different from what it was in the period 1960-73.

If the estimates used above are reasonably realistic, they raise two questions:

1. What will be the nature of the new type of development that can be expected?
2. What can be done in order to ensure that the rate of unemployment is really going down?

As regards the first question, it is worth noting that though the expected growth rate of labor productivity is much lower than for the earlier period, it is still positive. Though the estimates of *Interfutures* may be too optimistic, there is, on the basis of the present information, no reason to believe that the actual rate will be negative.

The new difficult period has already started. Tables 4.3 and 4.4 show some interesting features of the first five to six years after 1973. They reveal that investment has continued at roughly the level it reached in 1973 and that there has been a growth of labor productivity, though much slower than in the earlier period. This corresponds fairly well to the picture of the 1980s shown in the estimates quoted above. It must be added, though, that the negative effects of the oil price rises of 1979 and 1980 had not made themselves felt in the period covered by the two tables.

The trouble is that unemployment has remained at the high levels it reached after the first oil price rise. No improvement has taken place. The explanation of this fact is probably that the trend toward more and more capital-intensive and labor-saving methods of production has continued. The new equipment is more labor-saving than the equipment it has replaced. This was to be expected, because the real rates of interest are still extremely low—in fact, negative—for many investors in most countries. It is, therefore, profitable to replace labor by capital, just as before 1973.

This brings us to the second question raised above: What can be done to reduce unemployment if we get the rates of economic growth that can be expected? It should not be forgotten that the electronics revolution may bring about a new wave of labor-saving devices. It can have other consequences, such as increasing the demand for labor; but, as mentioned in the last part of Chapter 4, the net result is difficult to predict. Technological forecasting will be desirable in this, as in other fields regarding techniques that may be developed in the near future.

Such forecasts should be made under alternative assumptions concerning the relative prices of labor and capital. The relations between these prices will have a decisive influence on the nature of the new techniques that will be developed.

The answer to the question of what can be done to reduce unemployment thus lies to a large extent in the choice of technologies. In order to reduce the waste of labor now taking place, we should make the price relationship between labor and capital more realistic.

Real rates of interest are now often negative. But the true price of real capital is not negative. Investment requires real resources. One of these resources—energy—is now very expensive; and, as indicated in the previous section, the real prices of some raw materials may be rising in the foreseeable future. This is why the real rates of interest should again become positive, as described in the subsection "Capital Markets" in this chapter.

The adjustment to lower rates of economic growth does not require a drastic change in methods of production, but it requires a trend that is different from that of 1960-73. We cannot increase investment as fast as was done in that period. And of the investment that will be possible, increasing parts will have to be devoted to energy conservation, energy production, and improvements of the environment. On the other hand, the supply of labor will be ample in the 1980s, and it should be utilized. Techniques should therefore be less capital-intensive and labor-saving than in the 1970s. This requires a realistic and flexible fixing of the prices of labor and capital so that the demand for labor can be adjusted better to the available supply than in the recent past. Labor must, on the whole, become cheaper compared with capital.

CONCLUDING REMARKS

Four conclusions are the main results of this study of the problems of inflation and unemployment:

1. There should be an increasing internationalization of price control. Transnational price fixing, including the transfer pricing of multinational corporations, should be controlled to the greatest extent possible.
2. There should be wage policies consistent with the aim of approaching price stability. Governments should be responsible, in close contact with labor market organizations.

3. There should be increasing wage earner participation in the profits and owned capital of enterprises. The barriers between labor and capital should gradually disappear.
4. The real rates of interest should become positive for all investors, so that demand for labor can be stimulated in comparison with demand for capital.

The other suggestions made in this book are directly or indirectly, related to these four conclusions. The philosophy behind them is that the modern organization of markets, in its present form, contributes to inflation and unemployment. It should, therefore, be made more harmonious and coordinated.

The first conclusion deals with product markets, the two next with labor markets, and the last with capital markets. Among them they should make the whole system more harmonious and coordinated. The difficult task of establishing a wage policy should be facilitated if progress can be made concerning the other three conclusions, all of which will improve the situation of wage earners.

Progress regarding conclusions 1 and 4 requires international cooperation. Because of the growing economic interdependence of countries, there is a need for progress in the coordination of policies. In difficult matters too many countries should not be involved in the first instance. As regards conclusions 1 and 4, I hope leadership can be expected from major Western countries, such as the United States, Japan, Germany, the United Kingdom, and France. Progress regarding conclusion 1 has already been made by the European Communities.

The question may be asked whether progress on the lines suggested above will make our societies more complicated. The answer to that question is not simply yes or no. The proposals should be seen as integral parts of an effort to cope with problems that political authorities cannot escape taking up for solution.

Both our national societies and the international community are complicated today. They have become more complicated in recent years, partly because of inflation and unemployment. The present rates of unemployment are unacceptable, and the present rates of inflation are dangerous in many countries. Serious efforts will be needed to tackle these problems better than has been done until now.

If, on this background, we look at the four conclusions above, I think it is fair to make the following remarks:

Conclusion 1 will raise some problems and create complicated systems of control. But it should not be very difficult to extend a system similar to that of the European Communities to the United

States and Japan. Transfer pricing of multinational enterprises is already a subject of international discussion and investigation. And it will be easier to get wage policies accepted if it becomes known that something is done to limit the market power of strong multinational corporations.

Conclusion 2 is politically difficult, but it will not make the procedures of wage fixing appreciably more complicated than they are today.

Conclusion 3 can be handled in different ways. Where legislation is needed, systems can be defined that are not very complicated. And, in the longer run, progress in this field should counteract unrest in the labor markets and facilitate wage negotiations.

Conclusion 4 will require negotiations concerning monetary policy among the leading Western countries. But if they can agree, it should not be more difficult to administer the monetary systems, if the rates of interest are to play a greater role than they do today and the role of setting a target for the stock of money is reduced.

It must be added that if we can make real progress in these four fields, we will come much closer to price stability and full employment. This being so, it will be possible gradually to abolish the new protectionism and the individual systems of support to enterprises that have been introduced. These systems have primarily been substitutes for an adjustment of the economies to changing external conditions. Or they have been introduced because the cost level of the country has become too high.

This means that in various ways societies can become less complicated if the problems of inflation and unemployment are tackled in the ways suggested above.

If progress can be made concerning wage earner participation in profits and in owned capital of enterprises, it can help to resolve one of the most serious problems of modern societies, the conflict between the representatives of labor and capital. This is not only a labor market problem. It has also, in many countries, created dividing lines in political life that complicate the functioning of the systems. If progress can be made in this field, it should facilitate realistic wage negotiations so that the tasks of governments would become easier.

NOTES

1. See OECD, *Export Cartels* (Paris: OECD, 1974).

2. OECD, *Restrictive Business Practices of Multinational Enterprises* (Paris: OECD, 1973).

3. Jacques J. Polak, *The Per Jacobsson Lecture* (Washington, D.C.: The International Monetary Fund, 1979).

4. See Bruce Stokes, *Worker Participation—Productivity and the Quality of Work Life*, (Washington, D.C.: Worldwatch Institute, 1978).

5. OECD, *Monetary Targets and Inflation Control*, (Paris: OECD, 1979).

6. World Bank, *Annual Report 1979* (Washington, D.C.: World Bank, 1979), Statistical Annex, Table 1.

7. See Warren D. McClam, *US Monetary Aggregates, Income Velocity and the Euro-Dollar Market* (Basel: Bank for International Settlements, 1980), p. 43

8. International Monetary Fund, *Annual Report 1979* (Washington, D.C.: IMF, 1979), p. 43.

9. Anthony Edwards, *Raw Material Prices in the 1980s* (London: The Economist Intelligence Unit, 1977).

10. OECD, *Demographic Trends* (Paris: OECD 1979), p. 32.

11. OECD, *Interfutures* (Paris: OECD, 1979).

INDEX

ABOUT THE AUTHOR

THORKIL KRISTENSEN, professor of economics, is director of the Institute for Future Research and former president of the Academy for Research on the Future in Denmark. He is a former Member of Parliament and Minister of Finance in the Danish government, and from 1960 to 1969 he was Secretary-General of the Organization for Economic Cooperation and Development (OECD) in Paris.

Among his many publications are *The Economic World Balance, The Food Problem of Developing Countries*, and *Development in Rich and Poor Countries*.

Dr. Kristensen holds a Dr. Sc. Pol. (h.c.) from the University of Ankara.